SPIRITUAL REALITY

WITNESS LEE

Living Stream Ministry
Anaheim, CA

First Edition, July 2002.

ISBN 0-7363-1877-1

Published by

Living Stream Ministry
2431 W. La Palma Ave., Anaheim, CA 92801 U.S.A.
P. O. Box 2121, Anaheim, CA 92814 U.S.A.

Printed in the United States of America

02 03 04 05 06 07 08 / 10 9 8 7 6 5 4 3 2 1

CONTENTS

PREFACE

This book is composed of eighteen messages given by Brother Witness Lee in special edification meetings that were held in Taipei in August and September of 1954. These messages were not reviewed by the speaker.

Chapter One

GOD BEING SPIRIT

John 4:24 says, "God is Spirit, and those who worship Him must worship in spirit and truthfulness." Here the word *spirit* is mentioned twice: "God is *Spirit,* and those who worship Him must worship in *spirit* and truthfulness." Chapter six verse 63 reads, "It is the Spirit who gives life; the flesh profits nothing; the words which I have spoken to you are spirit and are life." This verse also mentions the word *spirit* two times. We see the principle that the Spirit gives life and that the words that the Lord speaks are spirit.

Chapter fourteen verses 17 to 20 say, "Even the Spirit of reality, whom the world cannot receive, because it does not behold Him or know Him; but you know Him, because He abides with you and shall be in you. I will not leave you as orphans; I am coming to you. Yet a little while and the world beholds Me no longer, but you behold Me; because I live, you also shall live. In that day you will know that I am in My Father, and you in Me, and I in you." Here it says that the Spirit will be with us. The world cannot receive or know this Spirit, but we the believers know Him, because He abides with us and shall be in us.

In verse 18 the Lord told the disciples that He would not leave them as orphans and that although He would leave, He would come back again. He also said that when He came back to in that day, He would live, and they also would live. Then they would know that the Lord is in the Father, and they are in the Lord, and the Lord is also in them. It is through the Holy Spirit that we are able to have these three "in"s. First John 4:13 states, "In this we know that we abide in Him and He in us, that He has given to us of His Spirit." The Holy

Spirit is the Spirit of God. When God gives us the Holy Spirit, there are two issues: one is that we abide in Him, and the other is that He abides in us.

John 3:6 says, "That which is born of the flesh is flesh, and that which is born of the Spirit is spirit." Here *spirit* is also mentioned twice: first, in the phrase *that which is born of the Spirit,* and second, in the expression *is spirit.* That which is born of a certain thing is that certain thing. Thus, that which is born of the Spirit is definitely spirit. We can also say that spirit can come only from the Spirit. God's salvation altogether depends on its spiritual reality; without spiritual reality, there would be no salvation of God. This is the same with our faith. Without the spiritual reality of faith, our faith would not exist.

CHRISTIAN LIVING DEPENDING ON THE SPIRIT

The Bible tells us that God is Spirit and that God became flesh. This indicates that God, who is Spirit, became flesh. The Lord Jesus is the God who is Spirit become flesh. We all know that the Holy Spirit is God Himself.

The innermost part of our being is our spirit. Our spirit as the center of our entire being is our reality. When we were saved, everything regarding salvation happened in our spirit. After we have been saved, our progress in life before the Lord is also a matter in the spirit. Thus, the progress of a Christian is the growth of a Christian in the spirit. Christian living, work, and even prayer all depend on the spirit.

In short, God, Christ, the Holy Spirit, the center of man, the reality of salvation, spiritual living, spiritual work, and even prayer are all in the spiritual realm. Only when we touch the spirit can we touch God, Christ, the presence of the Holy Spirit, the genuineness of man, the center of man, the salvation of God, and Christian progress. Hence, Christian living and function must be in the spirit in order to have reality. Without the spirit, all things are empty and are nothing but knowledge and doctrines.

THE ORIGIN OF THE SPIRIT BEING GOD

Every matter or thing has its origin, nature, and expression.

The spirit also has its origin, nature, and expression. First, the origin of the spirit is God. We know that gold often comes from the refined ore of a gold mine. Some of the ore contains the nature of gold, and through the refining process, gold is produced. Thus, the origin of gold is the gold mine. In the same way, because God is Spirit, the origin of the spirit is God Himself.

For example, if someone asks what a table is, we can say that the essence of a table is wood. If someone asks what man is, we can say that the essence of man is flesh and blood. If someone asks what a book is, we can say that the essence of a book is paper. Wood is the essence of a table, flesh and blood are the essence of man, and paper is the essence of a book. Every item has its essence, and its essence is based upon its origin. God is the origin, in God is an essence, and this essence is Spirit. This is what the Bible reveals to us.

GOD'S ESSENCE BEING SPIRIT

The Bible also says that God is love and light. God's being love denotes God's nature, and God's being light refers to His expression. However, these are not something of God's essence. For instance, if a lamp is not connected to the electricity, it will not shine. The shining of a lamp is the expression of electricity, but it is not the essence of electricity. We have never seen electricity, but we have seen the expression of the electricity—the shining of a lamp. The expression of electricity, however, is not the essence of electricity. Let us use another example. The heat that comes from an electric heater is the expression of the electricity but not the essence of the electricity. There is a distinction between the essence and the expression of a certain object.

It is difficult to explain the essence of the Spirit because no one has ever seen the Spirit. On the one hand, some Christians know the Spirit, but on the other hand, no Christian can see the essence of the Spirit, the Spirit Himself. Although we cannot see the Spirit, the Spirit manifests Himself in many ways. We can experience the presence of the Spirit, see the manifestation and power of the Spirit, and touch and contact the Spirit in the saints. According to the revelation of the

Bible, God is Spirit; the essence, the substance, of God is Spirit. When we say that God is with us, we mean that the Spirit is with us. God's being in us is the Spirit's being in us. When we fellowship with God, we are fellowshipping with the Spirit; when we touch God, we are touching the Spirit because God is Spirit. If we have the Spirit, we have God; if we lose the Spirit, we lose God. There is no God outside of the Spirit.

GOD CREATING A SPIRIT IN MAN
FOR MAN TO CONTAIN HIM

The Bible also reveals to us that it pleases God to mingle Himself with man. This is God's purpose in creating man. Genesis tells us that God created man in His image and according to His likeness (1:26) because the purpose of God's creation of man is that man would be a vessel to contain Him. For example, a Coca-Cola bottle is made to contain Coca-Cola. The appearance of a bottle indicates its purpose. The reason God created man exactly the same as He is is so that He may put Himself into man. However, the process through which God puts Himself into man is not that simple, because God is too mysterious. God as Spirit cannot put Himself into man, unless man has a spirit. Thus, the Bible tells us that when God created man, He not only created man in His image, but He also created a spirit in man (2:7; Zech. 12:1). How wonderful this is! God Himself is the uncreated, eternal Spirit, and in order for this uncreated, eternal Spirit to come into man, God created a spirit for man.

MAN HAVING THREE PARTS—
SPIRIT, SOUL, AND BODY

Hence, the man whom God created has three parts. The first part, the outermost part, is the body, which is visible, tangible, and physical. The second part is the soul, which is psychological, mental, and metaphysical. It can be divided into the mind, the emotion, and the will. The feelings of joy, anger, sorrow, and delight are all in the sphere of the soul. The third part, the innermost part of a person, is the spirit that God created for man. According to the revelation of the Scriptures, the conscience is a part of our human spirit.

MAN'S SPIRIT BEING SATISFIED
ONLY BY GOD

All the peoples of the world, whether civilized or barbarian, have the inclination and thought to worship God. While a person is in high school, owing to his youth, he may be very proud of himself and may never confess that there is God. After he goes to college, he may have an even higher opinion of himself, thinking that scholarship and knowledge are God. When he starts working, he may become more conceited, considering capability and reputation to be everything and absolutely neglecting God. However, when he has achieved success and acquired fame, there will be a change in his inner being. He will begin to feel that knowledge, capability, and reputation cannot satisfy him. There will also be a sense of emptiness within him that will become increasingly intense.

At this time, he may try to probe deeply into human life and to study human philosophy and religious ideology. Gradually, the inclination to worship God in his inmost being will become more pronounced. Some may worship a piece of stone, some may worship a piece of wood, and some may even worship a piece of paper. It seems that everything can be worshipped. Do not think that only uneducated people worship these things. In actuality, knowledgeable and highly educated people also do the same thing. Those who are thoughtful, knowledgeable, successful, and famous have an even greater need to worship God because although they have already reached the peak of their human life, they are still empty. The human spirit cannot be satisfied with knowledge, money, success, or reputation. Our body needs food and drink, our soul needs entertainment and enjoyment, and our spirit needs satisfaction. The human spirit needs nothing other than God Himself. God alone can be the unique satisfaction for the human spirit because it was created for the purpose of containing God.

The human spirit is the center of man, the genuineness of man, and the origin of all good in man. Man's heart of filial piety, sympathy, and compassion, man's conscience, and man's human virtues all come out of the spirit of man. The more a person cultivates and nurtures his spirit, the better and more virtuous he will be. If a person takes care only of his physical and psychological needs but overlooks his spiritual need, even though he may be a capable and knowledgeable person, he will most likely be a person who is short in morality. The spirit of man was created by God, who is the Father of lights, from whom are all good things (James 1:17). If a person gives his spirit its proper place in him, then he will be a person of supreme morality and will have the possibility to be a man above all men.

GOD WHO IS SPIRIT BECOMING FLESH

Man has a spirit which was created for God. God desires to put Himself into man, but sadly, man fell. Consequently, he does not know God and God's desire. Furthermore, he does not know that man was created for the purpose of receiving, containing, and mingling with God. So for the accomplishment of His eternal purpose, God decided to become flesh. This is the reason the Lord Jesus became a man. What is incarnation? John 1 says, "In the beginning was the Word, and the Word was with God, and the Word was God" (v. 1). The Word's becoming flesh (v. 14) is God's becoming flesh. The Lord Jesus is God who became flesh—God who is Spirit became flesh. Spirit is like electricity—unsubstantial, intangible, and abstract. Without electric lamps or electric fans, we would not be able to see electricity. When we see an electric lamp shining, we can say that we see the electricity in the shining. We can also say that the shining of the electric lamp is the "incarnation" of the electricity. Through the shining of the lamp, the electricity becomes something visible.

What is Christ? Christ is God becoming flesh. No one has ever seen God, but God became flesh—Christ. Christ is God becoming flesh, the embodiment of God. When He was among the disciples, outwardly He was almost the same as them, but inwardly there was a big difference. The difference was that the Spirit of God was in Him (cf. Luke 1:35; Matt. 12:28). The very Spirit of God was in Christ. Because God is Spirit, when

God became flesh, it was the Spirit who became flesh. Hence, Christ is the Spirit who became flesh.

SPIRITUAL REALITY

How can the Spirit who was in Christ enter into man? When Christ was on the earth, Peter, James, and John were always with Him, but He could not enter into them. Although they had seen His glory, tasted His love, and listened to His prayers and teaching, He could not enter into them. Thus, the Lord Jesus had to pass through death. Through death, the Lord came out of the constraint of His flesh and became the life-giving Spirit. Today Christ is the Spirit who is omnipresent. In every place, when He touches man, His Spirit touches and enlivens the human spirit. His touching man is His Spirit contacting the human spirit. Just like a radio receives the electric waves from the radio station, we all have the experience of contacting the Lord's Spirit with our human spirit.

No one can experience this for us. One day in the deepest part of our being—deeper than our mind, emotion, and will— something happened that made us feel unpeaceful and caused us to desire to kneel down to pray and confess, "O Lord, I am a sinner. I have offended my parents because I said something that I should not have said, and I have offended my colleague because I took something that I should not have taken. O Lord, I have sinned." At that time our tears came down, and we felt that our conscience within us was accusing us and forcing us to confess our sins and ask for the Lord's forgiveness. This is the experience of the pneumatic Christ entering into us, touching our spirit, and having such an effect on us. This effect was not something of our mind, emotion, or will but of the faith in our spirit. From that time on, this faith has become a genuine and living faith.

Therefore, we can see that spiritual reality is the God who is Spirit contacting our created spirit. The uncreated Spirit contacts the created spirit, and the two spirits fellowship with one another. This is spiritual reality.

CHAPTER TWO

THE KNOWLEDGE OF THE SPIRIT

John 6:63 says, "It is the Spirit who gives life; the flesh profits nothing; the words which I have spoken to you are spirit and are life." Here the Lord tells us that the words which He has spoken to us are spirit, meaning that the Word is spirit. John 14:17-20 says, "Even the Spirit of reality, whom the world cannot receive, because it does not behold Him or know Him; but you know Him, because He abides with you and shall be in you. I will not leave you as orphans; I am coming to you. Yet a little while and the world beholds Me no longer, but you behold Me; because I live, you also shall live. In that day you will know that I am in My Father, and you in Me, and I in you." On one hand, the Word is spirit, and on the other hand, the Spirit is the Spirit of reality.

Second Corinthians 3:17 states, "The Lord is the Spirit; and where the Spirit of the Lord is, there is freedom." Then verse 18 continues, "But we all with unveiled face, beholding and reflecting like a mirror the glory of the Lord, are being transformed into the same image from glory to glory, even as from the Lord Spirit." The Spirit is not only the Spirit of reality but also the Lord Spirit.

Ephesians 3:16-17 and 19 say, "That He would grant you, according to the riches of His glory, to be strengthened with power through His Spirit into the inner man, that Christ may make His home in your hearts through faith, that you, being rooted and grounded in love...may be filled unto all the fullness of God." This portion mentions three things—first, that God would grant us to be strengthened through His Spirit into our inner man; second, that Christ may make His home

in our hearts through faith; and third, that we may be filled
unto all the fullness of God.

THE SPIRIT OF GOD AND THE SPIRIT OF MAN
BEING MINGLED AS ONE SPIRIT

Spiritual reality hinges on the Spirit of God entering our
spirit and fellowshipping with our spirit. This is what produces spiritual reality. Spiritual reality originates from God's
desire, which is for Him to mingle Himself with man. God is
Spirit, and for the purpose of mingling Himself with man,
He created a spirit in man. The human spirit is of the same
nature as the Spirit of God. Hence, the human spirit is a
vessel to receive the Spirit of God. The truth and the center of
the entire Bible is concerning God as the Spirit entering into
the human spirit to mingle with man as one spirit.

THE WORD BECOMING FLESH—
THE FIRST UNION OF GOD AND MAN

In the Old Testament, we can see that God has a desire, an
intention, which is for Him to enter into man and be joined to
man. However, such an intention was not realized in the age
of the Old Testament. It was not until the time of the New
Testament that God became flesh. Incarnation was the first
union of God and man. John 1:14 tells us that the Word
became flesh. This verse reveals two things—the Word and
the flesh—and also unveils that the Word and the flesh were
mingled to be one. Since the Word is God, and the flesh is
man, the Word becoming flesh is God becoming man. This
was the first union of God and man in the universe.

From the creation of Adam to the birth of the Lord Jesus is
a total of approximately four thousand years. In these four
thousand years, God greatly desired to achieve the goal of
entering into man and mingling Himself with man as one.
However, from Adam to John the Baptist, there was not a
proper man who could allow God the opportunity to enter into
him and mingle with him as one. This was the case until one
day when something happened in Bethlehem—the God who
is the Word became flesh, entered into a man, and became a

man. The baby Jesus who was lying in the manger was the issue of God's mingling with man.

THE LORD JESUS BEING
THE MINGLING OF GOD AND MAN

Jesus was very mysterious. Outwardly speaking, He was indeed a man, but inwardly He was truly God. God's mingling with man began with this God-man Jesus Christ. He was the first man who had God mingled with Him. Many historians know that the man Jesus was special, but they do not know how or why He was special. The reason that the God-man Jesus was special is that God was in Him and was mingled with Him. Although He was a man, God was mingled with Him. He was special because of God.

When the Lord Jesus was walking on the earth, He asked those around Him, "Who do you say that I am?" (Matt. 16:13, 15). Surprisingly, those around Him also asked the same question concerning Him. They asked, "Who is He? Who is He really?" He asked people this question, and they also were asking the same question. The Lord Jesus was truly a mystery. He was born from His mother's womb with flesh and blood, and outwardly speaking, He was the same as everyone else—He shed tears, He grieved, He suffered pain, and He experienced sorrow, exhaustion, hunger, and thirst. In all these things He was exactly the same as other people. However, there was something mysterious about Him—He had surpassing power and wisdom, His words were beyond human imagination, and His character and morality were many, many times higher than that of others. While many people were astonished when hearing Him speak and wanted to hear Him more, others marveled at His acts and wondered who He really was. People asked questions like, "How can this man have such wisdom?" "How can He speak this word of authority?" "Is He not the son of a carpenter?" "Is He not from a small town of Nazareth?" The Lord was a man whose visage and form were marred, yet He was able to calm the winds and the sea, cause the dead to be raised, cause the blind to see, and cause the dumb to speak (Isa. 52:14; Matt. 8:26; 11:5). Who was this man?

The Lord Jesus was the first man who had God mingled with Him. He was the mingling of God and man, and because of this His wisdom was God's wisdom, His power was God's power, His authority was God's authority, and His acts were the expression of God. Sadly, however, those who were beside Him did not know him. The highest human evaluation of Him was that He was the greatest of the prophets. No one knew that this Jesus the Nazarene was a God-man, a man who was the mingling of God and man.

One day when He told His disciples that He had to leave them, one of the disciples said to Him, "Lord, show us the Father and it is sufficient for us" (John 14:8). The Lord was surprised by this request and asked, "Have I been so long a time with you, and you have not known Me, Philip? He who has seen Me has seen the Father....Do you not believe that I am in the Father and the Father is in Me?" (vv. 9-10). What the Lord meant when He said this was, "You see Me as a man, but God is inside of Me. We two—God and I—are one. When you see Me, you see God, because God and I are one. Apart from Me, you cannot find God, because God is in Me." When the Lord Jesus was on the earth, outwardly He was a man, but inwardly He was God mingled with man.

THE LORD BEING SPIRIT

When Jesus Christ was on the earth, outwardly He was a man, and inwardly He was God. Thus, since God is Spirit, the content of the Lord Jesus is Spirit, and since the Spirit gives life, as the Lord told the disciples, the words which the Lord spoke are spirit and are life (6:63). Why are the Lord's words spirit? A person's words are his representation, his expression. Since the Lord Jesus is God, He is also the expression of God, the Word of God, and as the Word of God, His words are spirit.

John 1:1 reads, "In the beginning was the Word, and the Word was with God, and the Word was God." Who was this Word? This Word was Christ Jesus. John 1:18 says, "No one has ever seen God; the only begotten Son [Christ Jesus], who is in the bosom of the Father, He has declared Him." Words are the declaration and the expression of man, the expression of the content of man. Why are the Lord's words spirit? It is because the Lord Himself is the Spirit. The Lord's words are the expression of the Lord, and the Lord is Spirit within. Thus, what comes out of the Lord is also spirit. The Lord's words are spirit because the Lord's words are the expression of the Lord Himself.

THE LORD BEING RESTRICTED IN THE FLESH

When the Lord was on the earth, although inwardly He was Spirit, outwardly He was flesh, a Nazarene. As such, the Spirit within was restricted by the flesh without. Because of this flesh, the Lord was limited not only by time but also by space. When He was in Jerusalem, He could not be in Samaria, and when He was in Judea, He could not be in Galilee at the same time. In fact, it was neither time nor space that limited Him; He was limited by His flesh. If He would have broken through the flesh, He would not have been bound by time or space. Spirit is beyond time and space. God is eternal; He is outside of time and space. However, when God became flesh, the flesh became His limitation. Hence, when the Lord Jesus was on the earth, He still could not enter into men. At most, He could be among men and face to face with men; He could not enter into them or mingle with them to be one, because He was under the restriction of the flesh. It was because of this restriction that He told His disciples that He would pass through death and be raised (Luke 9:22).

THE LORD BRINGING MAN INTO GOD
THROUGH RESURRECTION

What is the significance of the Lord Jesus' being raised from the dead? People in general think that the Lord Jesus died to shed His blood for us so that our sins would be forgiven, and that He was resurrected because He was the powerful Savior and could not be held by death. However, the true significance of the Lord's death and resurrection is more than this. Through death and resurrection, the humanity that the Lord had put on was put to death, passed through resurrection, and was brought into the glory of God (24:26; John 12:23-24). In His incarnation, the Lord put on a finite man. In His death and resurrection, He brought this finite man through death and resurrection and returned with this man into the glory of God. When He appeared to His disciples after His resurrection, He was the Spirit, but He also had a body—the marks of the nails, which were still on His hands, and the mark of the spear, which was still on His side, could be touched by Thomas (20:24-28). This proves that after the Lord's resurrection, He still had a human body, but that this body was not a body of the old creation. The Bible records that after His resurrection the disciples were meeting together in a certain place. Although all the doors and windows were shut, the Lord came and stood in their midst (vv. 19-23). A body in the old creation surely could not have done this.

In the resurrection of the Lord Jesus, that humanity that He had put on in His incarnation was brought into glory (Luke 24:26). This brought man into God because only God Himself is glory. His incarnation brought God into man, and His death and resurrection brought man into God. His coming and going were His incarnation, death, and resurrection. Jesus' coming to the world was God entering into man. Christ's resurrection was man entering into God.

THE LORD JESUS BEING GOD AND ENTERING INTO MAN THAT MAN MAY ENTER INTO GOD

In this universe there is a prototype that has been successfully produced—the God-man, the man-God, Jesus the Nazarene. Jesus the Nazarene was man yet God, God yet man. He was God entering into man, and man entering into God. He was the God who originally had no part in humanity and was the uncreated, eternal Spirit. One day this God put on humanity and for thirty-three and a half years mingled with man as one. This caused man to have the divine nature and God to have the human nature. These two were mingled but were not exchanged. He brought God into man and was hidden in a man for thirty-three and a half years, mingling divinity with humanity. Divinity and humanity were mingled together, but humanity had not yet been mingled into divinity. For this reason, the Lord Jesus needed further processing. As a man He needed to pass through death and resurrection.

Once He passed through death and resurrection, He brought humanity into divinity. The finite man now became infinite, and what was once limited by time and the space of the universe surpassed the limit of time and space. This was the accomplishment of Christ's incarnation, death, and resurrection. He was God entering into man, and man entering into God.

THE LORD BEING THE SPIRIT

The God who was uncreated and eternal, through incarnation, brought God into man, and through death and resurrection brought man into God. After the Lord's resurrection, the Bible calls Him the Spirit. The Lord who became flesh, who died and resurrected, and who was glorified is now the Spirit (1 Cor. 15:45b; 2 Cor. 3:17). The definite article—the—in the Greek text of 2 Corinthians 3:17 indicates that the Spirit is the unique Spirit in the universe. The Spirit is God Himself, and the Lord is the Spirit. The Spirit referred to here, however, is different from the uncreated, eternal Spirit, because in this Spirit referred to here there is both divinity and humanity. Andrew Murray once said that there is both divinity and humanity in the glorified Spirit. The Lord being the Spirit is one of the accomplishments of the Lord becoming flesh, dying, and resurrecting.

SPIRITUAL REALITY DEPENDING ON THE SPIRIT

Today Jesus is both in the heavens and on the earth. He is omnipresent because He is the Spirit. He is the Spirit, so He is beyond time, space, and all things in the universe from eternity to eternity. When as the Spirit He comes into contact with a person's spirit, that person is saved. Everything having to do with the spirit and all spiritual reality hinges on the contact and mingling of the Spirit with our spirit.

During China's War of Resistance against Japan, there was a man who was known for being ferocious. He was so mean that no one dared to approach him. However, one day this changed, and he told everyone joyfully, "The Lord Jesus has saved me." Formerly, this person was so evil that he was very cruel even to his mother. But one day he heard the gospel, and mysteriously, he began to have a lack of peace within him. He began to feel that he was a person who did not honor his mother, and all the scenes in which he had treated his mother cruelly flashed before his eyes. One night he cried without control. The next day he knelt before his mother, telling her in tears, "Mother, I am rebellious and incurable, but today the Lord Jesus has entered me and given me the feeling that I have failed you." People who saw this man weep were able to see in his tears that he had changed and was not the same. Why did he change? He changed because he received the Lord's Spirit into his spirit, and when the Lord's Spirit touched his spirit, he received the feeling, the consciousness, of life. This consciousness of life enabled him to realize his wrongdoings and confess to his mother. This is the story of many Christians. This is also spiritual reality.

The Lord in whom we believe is living. When we believe in Him, His Spirit stirs within us and touches our spirit. This brings about a response, an action, which may be to repent or confess. This response is expressed in a simple way in a person's living and is not something that we can outwardly demand of him or place upon him as a restriction. The genuine Christian living is something that comes from the living Christ, the living Spirit, who enters into man, touches man's spirit, and lives out from him. This produces an expression, which before man is love and before God is fear and spirituality. This is spiritual reality.

THE IMMEASURABLE SPIRIT
BEING GREATER THAN THE WORLD

We should never say that to be a Christian is a suffering. It is true that we have to rid ourselves of drinking, smoking, favoritism, and bribery, and that we must also honor our parents and love our neighbors. To do these things may be truly a suffering. We have to know, however, that genuine Christians do all these things not by outward regulation or teaching but by the inner power of life. History tells us that in the two thousand years of church history, because of this living Spirit, the more that Christians have suffered persecution, the stronger they have been inwardly. This is because even if the whole universe were to rise up to oppose the Spirit, it would not be able to overcome Him. Over these two thousand years there have been many kings who have persecuted Christians and the church. However, today all these kings have passed away, and the church is still here. The God of creation becomes a living power in those who believe in Him. He will never be defeated, and whoever opposes Him will suffer. He is the living God, the One who is without measure.

Today this God is the Spirit who is living in us and is one with us. Since we have such a Spirit in us, there is no difficulty that we are unable to overcome. Since we have such a Spirit in us, there are no situations that we are unable to pass through. Thus, we have to say, Hallelujah! The God who is the Spirit is in us, and He is greater than the world (1 John 4:4).

CHAPTER THREE

THE SEVEN SPIRITS—
THE LAMPS, THE EYES, THE SPIRITS,
AND THE FIRE

THE SEVEN SPIRITS BEING SENT FORTH
INTO ALL THE EARTH

Hebrews 12:29 says, "For our God is also a consuming fire." Revelation 4:2-3a reads, "Immediately I was in spirit; and behold, there was a throne set in heaven, and upon the throne there was One sitting; and He who was sitting was like a jasper stone and a sardius in appearance." Verse 5 continues, "And out of the throne come forth lightnings and voices and thunders. And there were seven lamps of fire burning before the throne, which are the seven Spirits of God." This verse speaks of seven lamps of fire burning before the throne, which are the seven Spirits of God. Then chapter five verse 6 states, "And I saw in the midst of the throne and of the four living creatures and in the midst of the elders a Lamb standing as having just been slain, having seven horns and seven eyes, which are the seven Spirits of God sent forth into all the earth." This verse says that a Lamb was standing before the throne of God and that the Lamb has seven eyes, which are the seven Spirits of God. Chapter four tells us that the seven Spirits of God are the seven lamps of fire, but here it says that the seven Spirits are the seven eyes of the Lamb. This verse also tells us that these seven Spirits are sent forth into all the earth.

Revelation 1:13a reads, "And in the midst of the lampstands One like the Son of Man, clothed with a garment reaching to the feet." The lampstands in this verse refer to the churches. In the midst of the lampstands, the churches, there is One like the Son of Man. Then verse 14 follows, "And His head and hair were as white as white wool, as snow; and His eyes were like a flame of fire." Second Chronicles 16:9 says, "For the eyes of Jehovah run to and fro throughout all the earth to strengthen those whose heart is perfect toward Him." From this verse we can see that the eyes of Jehovah are running to and fro throughout all the earth.

THE AGE OF THE HOLY SPIRIT

On the one hand, Christ has ascended to heaven, but on the other hand, He has come to tens of thousands of people as the Holy Spirit. How can Christ be in heaven while at the same time be the Holy Spirit? We have to know that after the Lord's death and resurrection, the age of the Holy Spirit began. In other words, after the Lord ascended to heaven, He came to the earth through the Holy Spirit to reach all who believe in Him. Hence, from His ascension to His second coming, this period of time is called the age of the Holy Spirit.

How does the Lord work on the earth in the age of the Holy Spirit? We all know that after the Lord's ascension, the Holy Spirit descended. Today the Holy Spirit, who is omnipresent, is working in the hearts of thousands of people. He is like the electric radio waves that cover the whole earth. The Bible does not tell us much about the situation in heaven after the Lord's ascension. At the end of the four Gospels, there it says only that the Lord has ascended to heaven; as for the situation in heaven after His ascension or what He is doing in heaven, there is no detailed account. However, we must thank the Lord that there are two chapters in the Bible that specifically record the situation in heaven after the Lord's resurrection and ascension. These two chapters are Revelation 4 and 5.

THE LORD BEING WITH THE CHURCH
UNTIL THE CONSUMMATION OF THE AGE

The first three chapters of Revelation speak of the various situations of the churches. In the midst of the churches on the earth, Christ is walking as the Son of Man in the midst of the golden lampstands. How can the Lord Jesus walk in the midst of the golden lampstands? Today the church that we are in is one of the many golden lampstands. I deeply believe that the Lord is walking among us. However, how does He walk among us? The Lord is with the church, but we can neither see this with our eyes nor touch it with our hands. In Matthew 28 the Lord clearly promised that even though He would ascend to heaven, He would still be with the disciples. He promised that He would be with them not only for one time or in a temporary way but all the days until the consummation of the age—until the time that He comes back. Therefore, the Lord's being with His disciples after His ascension is from the time of His ascension until His coming again. This is the promise that the Lord personally gave to the disciples at His ascension. Since He made such a promise, He surely will fulfill it. The situation of the church over the past two thousand years testifies that the ascended Lord has never left the church. He has been with the church the entire time.

Some people may ask, "How can the Lord be with the church? How can the Lord walk among the churches? Is He among us now?" Outwardly, we may say that the Lord is not with the church or with us because we cannot see Him or touch Him. However, the Lord clearly said that He is with the church. On the day the apostle John was on the island of Patmos, he saw the vision of the seven golden lampstands, which refer to the seven churches. We say that the church is a lampstand because a lampstand is a luminary that shines in darkness, and the church is a shining lamp in this age of darkness. In this world of darkness, the church is shining as a lamp, and Jesus Christ is walking in the midst of these seven lampstands, the churches. The apostle John saw this vision. Hence, not only did the Lord promise that His presence would be with the church, but the apostle John also saw it.

Revelation 4 and 5 show us the Christ in heaven, and the first three chapters of Revelation show us the Christ in the church. The Christ in the church is the Christ in heaven. Today the Christ on the earth is in the midst of His churches. Therefore, on the one hand, Christ is in heaven, and on the other hand, Christ is on earth, walking among His churches.

THE SEVEN SPIRITS OF GOD

After the apostle John saw the vision of the church, he saw the scene in the heavens. The first thing he saw was the throne as the center of the universe (4:2). He saw the throne in heaven, and upon the throne God was sitting and administrating the whole universe. The throne of God is the center of the universe; everything that happens in the universe begins at the throne. In John's vision, out of the throne came forth lightnings and thunders (v. 5). This shows that everything that happens in the universe is governed by the throne. There were seven lamps of fire burning before the throne. When a car is running at night, it requires two headlights, and the two headlights are like the two eyes of the car. Similarly, at the center of the universe, the throne of God, there are seven lamps of fire. God is Spirit, and the seven lamps of fire that come out of the throne of God are the seven Spirits of God.

Upon reading this portion of the Word, some people may ask, "Does God have seven Spirits? God is the Triune God. The Father, the Son, and the Spirit are one God. God is one, and He is Spirit, so the Spirit is also one. Since this is the case, why then does Revelation speak of the seven Spirits of God?" Revelation speaks of the seven Spirits of God because there are seven lamps of fire shining before the throne, and the lamps are the Spirit, so these seven lamps of fire are the seven Spirits of God. Hebrews 12:29 says that our God is a consuming fire. On the one hand, God is Spirit, and on the other hand, God is a consuming fire. The Spirit can be likened to electricity. Like electricity is expressed in a lamp, the Spirit shines through each lamp as fire. Hence, these lamps are lamps of fire. The Bible says that God is Spirit and also that God is a consuming fire. God's shining forth is a lamp of fire, and this lamp of fire is His Spirit. This picture in Revelation shows us that the God who is Spirit is also the God of consuming fire and that when this God comes forth in His Spirit, He is a lamp of fire shining upon man and the universe. When the seven lamps of fire before the throne of God eventually shine upon the entire universe, the darkness in the universe will vanish.

THE SEVEN LAMPS, THE SEVEN EYES,
THE SEVEN SPIRITS, AND THE CONSUMING FIRE

Revelation 4 reveals that since God is a consuming fire, His shining forth is like a lamp. In chapter five there is a Lamb before the throne of God, and this Lamb has seven eyes. Verse 6 includes the statement, "Seven eyes, which are the seven Spirits of God." The seven eyes of the Lamb are the seven Spirits of God. This means that God in the Lamb comes forth through the Spirit. First, we see the throne and the coming forth of God Himself as the Spirit, who is a consuming fire and lamps of fire. This is the first picture. Then we see that between God and the seven lamps of fire stands a Lamb who has seven eyes and that these seven eyes are the seven lamps of fire, the seven Spirits. Revelation 4 and 5 mention three "sevens." Chapter five mentions that the seven eyes of the Lamb are the seven Spirits of God, and chapter four says that the seven lamps of fire are also the seven Spirits of God. Together these two chapters mention the seven lamps of fire, the seven eyes, and the seven Spirits. The seven lamps in chapter four are the seven Spirits, and the seven eyes in chapter five are also the seven Spirits. Hence, the seven lamps in chapter four are the seven eyes in chapter five. The seven lamps before the throne are the seven eyes of the Lamb. The two are one. Both are the seven Spirits of God.

When we read Revelation, we cannot read it literally; rather, we have to read it like we would a poetic, idyllic painting. Revelation 4 shows us a picture of the throne. Out of the throne come forth the seven lamps of fire, the seven Spirits of God. Then in chapter five, we see that in the midst of the throne there is "a Lamb standing as having just been slain" (v. 6). *As having just been slain* refers to death, and *standing* refers to resurrection. The fact that the Lamb who is described as having just been slain is standing in the midst of the throne shows us that although He had just been slain, He also had been resurrected. The Lamb also has seven eyes, and these seven eyes are the seven Spirits of God. Thus, we can see that the seven lamps are the seven eyes of the Lamb. This indicates that when God shines Himself forth, He is seven lamps of fire and that when Christ diffuses the shining forth of God, He is the seven eyes of the Lamb. We also see that these seven eyes are the seven Spirits of God.

THE ISSUE OF THE SPIRIT OF GOD REACHING MAN AND HAVING A RELATIONSHIP WITH MAN

Fire is fearful, but if fire becomes a lamp, it is no longer fearful. Moreover, if the lamp becomes an eye, it is even less fearful. The eyes are the most attractive part of a person's countenance. Our God is a consuming fire, but when He comes to have a relationship with man, and when He comes forth through His Spirit, He is like a lamp of fire that shines on us and is to us whatever we need. Moreover, after Christ's death and resurrection, He ascended to God, and His seven lamps became the seven eyes, which are the seven Spirits of God. Revelation further tells us that these seven Spirits are sent forth into all the earth. In other words, the seven Spirits are the seven eyes of the Lamb, the seven eyes of the Lamb are the lamps of the fire of God, and the lamps of the fire of God are the consuming fire of God, which is God Himself. The fire shines forth from the lamps, the lamps are diffused through the eyes, this diffusion is the Spirit of God, and the Spirit of God is sent forth into all the earth. This is what is revealed in Revelation 4 and 5.

This is the process by which the Spirit of God enters into man to have a relationship with man. We must be clear that on the one hand, God is Spirit, and on the other hand, God is a consuming fire. When He comes forth, He comes forth in the way of shining, not in the way of burning. Not only so, God also has passed through death and resurrection to become the seven eyes of the slain and resurrected Lamb. Whomever the Lamb sees, He shines upon and reaches as the Spirit, who is sent forth into all the earth. Whomever the Spirit visits, God enlightens, and whomever the Spirit enlightens, God reaches. Hence, when God reaches man, He comes as the Spirit to care for man and the fire to enlighten man.

This is the process through which God works on the earth after Christ's resurrection. For example, before a brother encounters any particular difficulties in his life, he may never think about the Lord or love the Lord. He may remain cold toward the Lord, sometimes attending the meetings and sometimes not attending the meetings. Though he may not commit any great mistakes, his condition may remain somewhat abnormal. One day, however, if this brother encounters a big problem that he is unable to handle, he may spontaneously have the feeling within that the eyes of God are looking at him. If he does have this experience, his inner being will be enlightened, and because of this light, he will have the inner sense that he has committed certain mistakes. When we pray and fellowship with the Lord in the morning, we often have this kind of feeling within—the feeling that God's eyes are looking directly at us from the throne. The look from God's eyes is bright and radiant. It awakens us and warms us up. All saved ones have had this kind of experience.

THE PROCESS OF GOD'S BEING WITH MAN

If we visit someone, this means that we care for him. If we do not care for someone, we will not look at him or visit him. When we care for someone, we begin by looking at him. Then once we look at him, we are full of feeling for him, and when our feeling is expressed to him, he will have a sense of warmth and will feel happy that we have visited him. When we are in the midst of a difficult situation and are without a way to get out of it, within us there is a beam of light connecting us to heaven, where there are eyes looking at us from the throne. The eyes that are looking at us are like shining lamps of fire. God's looking is His shining. By this looking and shining, we are enlightened, and we sense what we have done wrong and sense in which matters we have sinned. The result of our being enlightened is that we immediately sense that the Holy Spirit is moving within us and filling us. Once the Holy Spirit moves within us and fills us, He is like a fire burning within us. The eyes look at us, the lamps of fire enlighten us, and the Holy Spirit comes to visit us. When the Holy Spirit comes to visit us, He is like a consuming fire. This is the process by which God works on us and in us today.

This is why in our experience we are able to sense that there are always eyes looking at us from the throne. When we are having morning revival or reading the Bible, and even

when we are indifferent toward God, strangely, the eyes from
the throne are looking at us. They are invisible, yet they seem
almost visible. We can definitely sense that there are eyes in
heaven looking at us, lamps of fire shining upon us, and the
Holy Spirit moving in us, filling us, and burning within us.
We experience the looking, the shining, the filling, and the
burning. When all these experiences come to us, we sense
that we are full of the presence of God, full of the presence of
Christ.

While I was at a summer camp in 1932, one morning after
everyone had gone to the meeting, I stayed behind in my
room and studied a spiritual book. After reading a particular
sentence, although outwardly I did not feel that I had been
greatly affected by it, inwardly I had the sense that I was
connected to the throne in heaven and that there were eyes
looking at me from the throne. Eventually, I could not read
my book anymore. I stopped and looked up at the ceiling, and
as I did so, inwardly I saw into the heavens. I clearly sensed
within that there were eyes looking at me, calling me, and
saying to me, "Turn to Me," so I put my book aside and said
within myself, "O Lord, You are right. I must turn to You."
Once I said this, I was no longer able to sit peacefully, so I
stood up. When I stood up, I sensed that the eyes in heaven
were still looking at me. Then I said within myself again,
"O Lord, You are right. I must turn to You." After saying this,
the feeling within me became stronger, so I knelt down before
my bed and prayed, "O Lord, You are right. I must turn to You."
After praying this, I was enlightened within, and I prayed to
the Lord based on this shining. The more I prayed, the more
I sensed the filling of the Holy Spirit, and the more joyful I
became. I felt like I was being burned by fire, and there was
an energy driving me from within.

As I prayed in my room that day, I did not know what
realm I was in. I simply sensed that I was directly before God.
As I prayed with my eyes closed, I felt that God was in the
room. Inwardly I was touching God and was connected to the
heavens. I did not know why, but at that time I simply sensed
a sweetness within, so I prayed, "O Lord, I do not want the
world; I just want to follow You. I want to be a preacher."

As I went home after the summer camp had ended, I felt like I was flying. From that time on, my mother, my wife, my brother, and my sister-in-law would often say, "This person is captivated. Even while he eats, his eyes are looking toward the heavens. Look at how joyful he is!" I was full of joy every day, and there was a fire burning within me.

I had this experience at the end of June in 1932, and in the middle of July, two weeks later, God worked in the environment and sent someone to look for me and meet with me. On one Thursday we had four people meeting together, a week later ten met with us, and on the third week eleven of us met together for the Lord's table. During that time I was living in the heavens. I was filled with joy, and there was a fire burning within me every day. In that period of time I did not dare to sing hymns on the love of the Lord Jesus, because whenever I sang hymns about the Lord's love, I shed tears, and whenever I sang hymns about the death of the Lord Jesus, I wept. I continually had the inward sense that there were still so many people who did not know the Lord's death and had not received the Lord's love. This experience, in which such a fire burned within me, is beyond description.

Those who are in such a situation do not need anyone to exhort them to love God and man and to not love the world. The fire within them will burn in them and make them humble and meek. They will not only love people but will also bring them to salvation. Our experience of the presence of God begins with the eyes from heaven looking at our inner being. This is the shining of the lamps of fire. Then when the lamps of fire shine in us, they burn within us, and the Spirit moves in us. Eventually, the fire is both the lamp and the Spirit, and the Spirit is God Himself. This is the process by which God is with us.

A CHRISTIAN'S LIVING, PATH, AND EVERYTHING COMING FROM THE SHINING AND BURNING OF THE SPIRIT OF GOD

During China's War of Resistance against Japan, I was imprisoned by the Japanese for preaching the gospel in Northern China. While I was in prison, I prayed every day. The

Japanese put me into a cell together with a Greek man. This man belonged to the Greek Orthodox Church, and we enjoyed our conversations very much. When he asked me why I had been imprisoned, I told him that I had been imprisoned for preaching Jesus. For this reason, he respected me very much and asked me to pray with him regularly. Twenty days later he was released, and I was left alone. On that day I knelt down to pray by myself. Once I knelt down, the eyes in heaven shone on me like a beam of light. Tears fell from my eyes, and a hymn welled up within me. As I began to sing, I felt that the Lord was right there with me. I was inwardly connected to the heavens, and I did not have any feeling of loneliness or suffering. At that time, even though I was in prison, I was full of praises and joy as though I were in the heavens.

This experience was not the result of someone exhorting or teaching me; rather, it was the result of God in heaven shining into me through His Spirit, His eyes, to motivate me with the light and energy of His fire. This is the source of a Christian's living. A Christian does not live by outward imitation but by the shining of the Spirit of God into him. We can say that this shining is the eyes, the lamps, the fire, or the Spirit. In short, God is the Spirit, and He is also a consuming fire. When He comes to us, the first thing He does is to look at us with His eyes. When He sees us, He shines on us, when He shines on us, He burns us, and when He burns us, He motivates us within. This is spiritual reality, and this is the Christian living.

In the past there was a female preacher in China whose name was Dora Yu. When she was around twenty years old, she decided to study medicine in England. On the day that her ship was approaching Marseilles, the Spirit of God reached her and burned in her. She sensed a voice within her, saying, "Go back! Go back! Do not go to England to study medicine." The year that this happened was toward the end of the Ching Dynasty. At that time, for a young lady who had been sent by her parents to England to study medicine to have such a feeling in the middle of her voyage was unthinkable. Nevertheless, she said to the captain, "I must land. I will not go to England." Upon hearing this, the captain asked her,

"What are you going to do when you go back to China?" She replied, "I have to go back to China to preach Jesus." The ship had to continue its voyage, so they landed her in France, and from there she went back to China. When her family came to pick her up, they thought that she must have returned because she was ill. When they found that she was not sick, they scolded her. In response she told them, "There was a fire burning in me; the Holy Spirit was moving in me continually, urging me to preach the gospel." No matter how much she explained, however, her parents still did not understand, and no matter how strongly her parents persuaded her, she could not be changed. Since her parents had no way to change her, they told her out of anger, "If Jesus wants you to preach Him, that is fine. We will go back home. You stay in Shanghai alone, and let Jesus take care of feeding you."

After her parents left her, Dora Yu was alone by herself. As she was looking to God, He opened the way for her and prepared a flat for her on Broadway in Shanghai. It was there that she began to preach the gospel, and from that time on God greatly used her. Those who were in Shanghai in 1948 testified that following Dora Yu's preaching every row of chairs in both the chapel and the hallway would be wet because of people's tears. Many wept, repented, and were saved by her preaching. In those days few in China preached concerning regeneration. Dora Yu may have been the first one. Today in Christianity there are many great servants of God who were saved through her preaching.

When God works in man, He looks into man's inner being. God's eyes are His lamps of fire, and when these lamps of fire shine within a person, there is a burning within him. This burning is the moving of the Spirit of God, and the Spirit of God is God Himself, Christ Himself. The living, the path, and everything of a Christian come from this burning. They do not come from the teaching without but from this burning within. This is spiritual reality.

CHAPTER FOUR

THE PURPOSE OF
THE WORK OF THE HOLY SPIRIT

GOD DESIRING TO BE MINGLED WITH MAN

Many of the divine revelations in the Bible are fulfilled in the book of Revelation, for the record in the book of Revelation is the conclusion of the entire Scriptures. The center of the entire Bible is that God wants to work Himself into man to the extent that He is fully mingled with man. In other words, He desires that His divinity would be mingled with humanity and humanity would be mingled with His divinity, so that God and man, man and God would be fully mingled as one.

Even though divinity and humanity are two entirely different natures, the work of God throughout all the generations is to work these two natures into one, that divinity may be in humanity, and humanity in divinity, to the extent that you would not be able to see God without seeing man or see man without seeing God. In the end, at the consummation of God's work, you will be able to smell humanity when you touch divinity and taste divinity when you touch humanity, because at that time God and man, man and God will be fully mingled as one. God will then be able to say that we are the same as He is, and we also will be able to say that God is the same as we are. At that time God and man will be in complete harmony. God and we, we and God will become fully one and will be inseparable. Apart from the Godhead, we will be one hundred percent exactly the same as God (cf. 1 John 3:2).

The first mention of man in the Bible is God's creation of man in His image (Gen. 1:26). Although man is man, he has the image of God. It is obvious from the Scriptures that in

God's heart, He wants to work in man to the point that man is exactly the same as He is. God's work in man to make man exactly the same as He is began in Genesis. From Genesis 2 on, God has been continually working. Even after His birth, the Lord Jesus still told us, "My Father is working until now, and I also am working" (John 5:17). This shows us that this work has not yet ceased and has not yet been accomplished.

THE NEW JERUSALEM BEING
THE TOTALITY OF THE WORK OF GOD

This work was not accomplished when the Lord Jesus was on the earth, and though the Holy Spirit descended almost two thousand years ago, this work is still not yet accomplished. God's work throughout the generations will not be accomplished until the day that the holy city, New Jerusalem, is manifested. This holy city, New Jerusalem, is the issue of God's work throughout the generations. The entire Bible reveals to us that the ultimate issue and product of God's work will be the New Jerusalem. What is the New Jerusalem? The New Jerusalem is the totality of God's work, the issue of God's work throughout the ages and generations. The glory, radiance, color, and appearance of the New Jerusalem are exactly the same as God in His glory, radiance, color, and appearance.

THE TRIUNE GOD—
THE FATHER, THE SON, AND THE SPIRIT—
BEING EXPRESSED ON THE THRONE

Revelation 4 shows us a picture of the image of God. This chapter says that there is a throne set in heaven and upon the throne there is One sitting. We all know that the One on the throne is God, because the seven Spirits which come forth out of the throne are the seven Spirits of God (v. 5). Moreover, in the midst of the One sitting on the throne and the seven Spirits which come forth out of the throne, is a Lamb standing as having just been slain (5:6). Who is the Lamb standing as having just been slain? He is Christ, the Son of God. The Divine Trinity—the Father, the Son, and the

Spirit—is expressed on and around the throne, comes forth out of the throne, and is sent forth into all the earth.

The One who is sitting on the throne is God, and God is both a consuming fire and Spirit (Heb. 12:29; John 4:24). In Leviticus 10, Nadab and Abihu came before God, but because they violated the statute of God, fire came out and consumed them (vv. 1-2). The Bible tells us that God dwells in unapproachable light (1 Tim. 6:16). This light, no doubt, comes out of the consuming fire. On the one hand, God comes out as Spirit, and on the other hand, He comes out as consuming fire. Hence, the seven lamps of fire that come forth out of the throne are the seven Spirits of God. Why are the seven Spirits of God seven lamps of fire before the throne? The seven Spirits are seven lamps of fire because God is a consuming fire, and what is diffused from Him must also be fire. The fire that is diffused from God is contained in lamps, so that God can approach man. If God were only the fire but not the lamps of fire, no one would dare approach Him. Thank the Lord that when He is diffused from His throne, He is lamps of fire, so that man may approach Him. The lamps of fire are God Himself. In addition, because God is Spirit, what is diffused from Him is also Spirit.

THE SEVEN SPIRITS, THE SEVEN LAMPS, AND THE SEVEN EYES

In Revelation 4 we see that the One who is on the throne is God, and the One who comes out of the throne is the Spirit. God the Father is on the throne, and God the Spirit is diffused from the throne. Inserted in chapter five is the Lamb standing as having just been slain. The seven eyes of this Lamb are the seven lamps of fire. Thus, we can say that the seven lamps of fire before the throne are the seven eyes of the Lamb, and the seven eyes of the Lamb are the seven Spirits. In other words, God the Father who is on the throne passes through God the Son—Christ who has been slain and resurrected—and is diffused. What goes out in this diffusion is not only the lamps of fire, which enlighten man, but also the seven Spirits who take care of man and are sent forth into all the earth. The seven Spirits can reach everywhere in all the earth.

The center of the universe is the throne. On this throne there is one God, and before this throne there are seven lamps, which are the seven eyes of God, the seven Spirits of God. These seven Spirits come out of God by shining and observing through Christ who was slain and resurrected. The shining and observing seven Spirits are sent forth into all the earth to observe everyone in every corner. Wherever the seven Spirits look, there is blessing and there is the shining of God's lamps of fire, and wherever God's lamps of fire shine, there is the burning of the fire of God. The fire of God is the Spirit of God, and the Spirit of God is God Himself. Wherever there are God's lamps of fire, there is the presence of God, and wherever there are God's lamps of fire, there is God Himself. Eventually, the result of the burning of the fire of God will be a group of people who are one hundred percent exactly the same as God.

Revelation 4:3a says, "And He who was sitting was like a jasper stone." This means that the One who is sitting on the throne is like jasper in appearance. In the entire Bible, God's image is seldom mentioned, but here it says that the One who is sitting on the throne has an image like a jasper stone. When the apostle John saw this vision, he seemed to declare that the One on the throne has the appearance, splendor, color, and radiance like that of a jasper stone. When God shines forth through Christ—the One who was slain and resurrected—He is the Spirit. He is also like eyes looking at man's inner being, and these eyes are God's lamps of fire. Wherever there is the shining of God's lamps of fire, there is the burning of fire, and wherever there is the burning of fire, there is the filling of the Spirit. In Acts, when the Holy Spirit descended on the day of Pentecost, He was like tongues of fire (2:3). The Lord Jesus also said that He came to cast fire on the earth (Luke 12:49). That fire is the Spirit of God, God Himself. When the Lord Jesus came, He brought God to the earth so that man may receive God. God in the Lamb is the lamps of fire and the flames, and both the lamps and the flames are the eyes.

THE GOD ON THE THRONE AND THE HOLY CITY, NEW JERUSALEM, BEING EXACTLY THE SAME

Our God is a consuming fire, but when He passed through Christ, He became lamps of fire and the eyes of the Lamb. After passing through Christ—the One who was slain—the consuming fire, which can burn man up, became the seven Spirits, the lamps of fire, and the seven eyes that enlighten and take care of us. The Holy Spirit's working in us is first to take care of us by observing us. When He observes us, we sense that He is like light that shines upon us. This shining gives us the feeling that we are being burned—everything that should not be in us is burned away and burned up. On the other hand, this fire within us also acts as a motivating power that drives us from within. This experience fills us with the presence of the Spirit. The Spirit is Christ, and Christ is God. Thus, when we are filled with the Spirit, we are filled with the element of God, and this element, which is God Himself, is a consuming fire. The result of such burning is that we have the splendor of God, the appearance of God, and the radiance of God so that we become exactly the same as God.

In Revelation we see that when God's work is completed, the New Jerusalem is produced. Moreover, we see also that the splendor, color, and radiance of the New Jerusalem are the same as that of God. Chapter four says that the God who is sitting on the throne is like a jasper stone (v. 3); chapter twenty-one goes on to say that the radiance and color of the New Jerusalem are also like a jasper stone (vv. 11, 18-19). Verse 11 reads, "Having the glory of God. Her light was like a most precious stone, like a jasper stone, as clear as crystal." This clearly indicates that the glory of the city is the glory of God, the light of the city is the light of God, the color of the city is the color of God, and the appearance of the city is the same as the appearance of God. The One who is sitting on the throne is like a jasper stone, and the expression of the holy city is also like a jasper stone. In the end the city and the One who is sitting on the throne are exactly the same, having no difference.

Revelation also reveals that the city itself is pure gold

(v. 18). This refers to the content and inner life of the redeemed ones. The content and inner life of the redeemed ones is the nature of God, God Himself. We can say this because in the Bible gold denotes the nature of God. All those who have been redeemed have the life of God, the nature of God, and God Himself within them, but do they all have the jasper wall, the splendor of God, without? This is an exceedingly great matter. The city itself is pure gold because it has the nature of God, but the wall of the city is jasper as a result of transformation. God operates in this city to build its wall. Thus, the city being jasper is the issue of God's operation and transformation.

THE JASPER WALL BEING THE SEPARATING BOUNDARY

The pearl gates of the city signify regeneration. Once we are saved, we enter through the pearl gates by regeneration. A pearl is produced when an oyster is wounded by a grain of sand. The oyster being wounded to produce a pearl signifies Christ being wounded by us and dying for us in order to make us pearls. Hence, the pearl gates signify our regeneration. As a result of being saved and regenerated, we have God's life, the pearl gates, and the street of pure gold in us, but the question is, do we have the jasper wall? A wall is a separating boundary, a powerful protection. Everything that belongs to the city is inside the wall, and all that does not belong to the city is outside the wall. The wall is the separating boundary.

Many saved ones, even though they have entered through the pearl gates and have the nature of pure gold within them, do not have the wall—the protection and separating boundary. They cannot tell what is of God and what is not of God, what pleases God and what displeases Him, or what God wants and what He does not want. They do not have the power of separation in their friendships, their work, or their career, because they lack a wall, a separating boundary. This separating boundary is the jasper wall, and jasper is the image of God. The separating boundary in us is our likeness to God. How much of the appearance of God we have determines how much separation we have. If our appearance of God is "two feet high," then the jasper wall in us will also be "two feet high." If the element of God increases in us by "three feet," then the separating boundary in us will also increase by "three feet."

THE ISSUE OF GOD'S WORK BEING TO MAKE MAN EXACTLY THE SAME AS HE IS

The issue of God's work is to produce such a separating boundary that acts as a wall within us. This wall is nothing other than the appearance of God. The wall and God are exactly the same in appearance. God on the throne is jasper, and the wall is also jasper. At the end of Revelation, the result of the completion of God's work is that all those who have passed through His work have the radiance of God and are the same as God. The result of God's work is a city with jasper as its wall. The radiance and color of the city are exactly the same as the One who is sitting on the throne.

The work of the Holy Spirit is to produce spiritual reality. The Holy Spirit is working in us continuously to work the image of God into us, and the result of this work is that we become exactly the same as God. God is jasper, and we also have jasper in us. This jasper becomes a wall, a separating boundary within us, and whenever anyone sees this separating boundary, they see the image of God. Whoever passes through the work of the Holy Spirit will be made to be exactly the same as God.

THE WORK OF GOLD, SILVER, AND PRECIOUS STONES

First Corinthians 3 tells us that a worker who is useful to the Lord must do the work of gold, silver, and precious stones instead of wood, grass, and stubble (vv. 12-13). This is the kind of work that the Triune God does within us, a work of gold, silver, and precious stones. God the Father is the golden nature. When His life and nature enter into us, this is the gold. The redemption of God the Son is the silver. The issue of the work of God the Spirit, the Holy Spirit, is the precious stones. Both gold and silver are created, but precious stones are produced through a process of burning, high heat, high pressure, and reconstitution. Hence, the precious stones signify the burning work of the Holy Spirit within us. The Holy Spirit who is within us puts us—those who were originally made of clay—into the fire of the Holy Spirit. After we have passed through the burning of the Holy Spirit, the result is precious stones.

THE WORK OF THE SEVEN EYES OF GOD

The One who is making us jasper is the jasper One on the throne. God's throne is His reigning, and out of His sovereign reigning comes forth fire (Rev. 4:5). The fire that comes out of His reigning, however, is not a consuming fire but lamps of fire to enlighten us. If God were merely a consuming fire, He would be fearful. However, since He is the lamps of fire, He is not fearful to us. We are always safe before a lamp. Moreover, the Lamb, Christ, who passed through death and resurrection has eyes that transfuse God and convey His feelings. One glance, or even one rebuke, from His eyes is full of feelings. The organs which most express a person's feelings are his eyes.

Christ came forth from the throne of God, which represents His sovereignty and reigning, as a consuming fire. But after passing through death and resurrection, He became lamps and eyes. Because of this, when we taste the visitation and grace of God, our first inner feeling is that God's eyes are looking at our inner being. Every time we come near to God in order to meet God, taking the precious blood of the Lamb who was slain, the God in heaven is not like thunder and lightning or a burning fire to us; instead, He is like eyes that look into our inner being. Every day when we come near to God in the Lamb who was slain, we have fellowship with God, and inwardly our first feeling is that God's eyes are looking into our inner being.

These eyes are also the Spirit of God. Every time we have fellowship with God, His eyes look at our inner being, for these eyes are sent forth into all the earth. Whenever we come near to God, this is our first experience. Our second experience is that we sense that God is enlightening us inwardly. The eyes are lamps of fire to enlighten us, causing us to know immediately that we are wrong in certain matters and to feel that we should deal with and resolve certain matters. First, the eyes look at us, and the result of this looking is the shining. Then the result of this shining is the burning of fire. The burning of fire, on the one hand, deals with everything that should not exist and, on the other hand, motivates us inwardly.

Through this kind of burning, we who were made of clay will become jasper. After one experience of the burning, we have more of the appearance of jasper; after another experience of the burning, we have the addition of the element of God; after another experience of the burning, we have more of the color of God; and after yet another experience of the burning, the appearance of God emerges. In one burning after another the eyes look at us, the lamps shine into us, and the burning comes to us. Through these experiences, we will have more of the appearance of God, and in our living we will have more of the expression of God in appearance and image.

SPIRITUAL REALITY

God who is sitting on the throne is a consuming fire and Spirit, and what comes out of Him is consuming fire, lamps of fire, the seven Spirits, and the eyes. When He looks at a person and shines into him, He burns in him, and the result is precious stone. How much appearance, radiance, and color of God can a man of clay have? Through the work of the Holy Spirit, a man of clay can be burned to the extent that he becomes part of the New Jerusalem. When this happens, this redeemed one will not only have entered the pearl gate and have the element of pure gold but will also have the issue of the burning of the Holy Spirit—the wall constituted with the Holy Spirit. This wall bears the appearance of God and is a separating boundary. Whenever we see this wall in a person, we see God's radiance, God's image, and a clear separating boundary.

This separating line discerns between what is heavenly and what is earthly, what is spiritual and what is fleshly, what is of God and what is of man, and what is holy and what is common. This discernment comes from the constitution of the Holy Spirit and is produced by the burning of the Holy

Spirit. It is by this discernment that the image of separation and the radiance of the Holy Spirit are expressed. The result is the reality of the Holy Spirit, which is spiritual reality.

CHAPTER FIVE

THE MIND, EMOTION, AND WILL BEING MADE SPIRITUAL

Romans 8:9-11 says, "But you are not in the flesh, but in the spirit, if indeed the Spirit of God dwells in you. Yet if anyone does not have the Spirit of Christ, he is not of Him. But if Christ is in you, though the body is dead because of sin, the spirit is life because of righteousness. And if the Spirit of the One who raised Jesus from the dead dwells in you, He who raised Christ Jesus from the dead will also give life to your mortal bodies through His Spirit who indwells you." This portion mentions three times that the Spirit of God dwells in us.

GOD WORKING THROUGH HIS SPIRIT

The work of God throughout all the generations has been to reach one goal, to mingle Himself with man and, through this mingling, to work in man to the extent that man becomes exactly the same as He is. Through His incarnation, God put His life into man that man would have the divine nature. Then through His death and resurrection, He brought His humanity into Himself, mingling humanity with His divinity. God's goal to mingle Himself with man is accomplished entirely through His Spirit.

God is Spirit. Thus, in order for Him to enter into man, He had to create a spirit in man (Zech. 12:1). Man's spirit is a vessel to contain God and an organ to contact Him (2 Tim. 4:22; John 4:24). The human spirit receives the Spirit of God and interacts with His Spirit, and the two become one (Rom. 8:16; 1 Cor. 6:17). Man's contact and relationship with

God are altogether not in the mind, emotion, or will but in the spirit. The Lord Jesus told us that God is Spirit and that those who worship Him must worship in spirit and truthfulness (John 4:24). Our worship of God does not depend on any outward place; it is the same here or there, inside or outside. What is crucial is our spirit. Because God is Spirit, we must contact Him in spirit.

JESUS CHRIST BEING GOD YET MAN

For the Spirit of God to enter into our spirit, Christ had to pass through incarnation, death, and resurrection. Christ's incarnation brought God into man, and Christ's death and resurrection brought man into God. This coming and going of Christ brought God into man and man into God. Christ who died, resurrected, and ascended is God with the human nature and man with the divine nature. He is God yet man and man yet God. Divinity and humanity have been completely mingled within Him as one.

THE ASCENDED CHRIST BEING
THE PROTOTYPE OF GOD'S GOAL

Today in the universe, the ascended Christ in the heavens is the prototype of God's goal. God's goal in the universe is to mingle Himself with man, and the resurrected and ascended Christ is God mingled with man. Divinity and humanity, humanity and divinity, are mingled within Him. The mingling of divinity and humanity within Him is the mystery of this resurrected and ascended Christ. Hence, today He is in the heavenlies as the prototype and model of God's goal. In addition to being the prototype of God's goal, after resurrecting and ascending, Christ sent the Holy Spirit (15:26). As the Holy Spirit, He comes into all those who believe in Him (14:15-18). Just as He passed through incarnation, death, and resurrection to bring God into man and bring man into God, now as the Holy Spirit, He is doing the work of incarnation in us—bringing God into us—and the work of death and resurrection in us—bringing us into God. From the time of our salvation, this principle of incarnation is applied to us.

THE HOLY SPIRIT BEING SENT FORTH
INTO ALL THE EARTH

After we are regenerated, the work of the Holy Spirit in us is to bring us through death and resurrection so that we will be mingled with God. God is in Christ, and Christ is in the Holy Spirit. Christ is not only God's mingling with man but also man's mingling with God. This model of mingling is entirely accomplished in the Holy Spirit, and as the One who accomplished this model of mingling, the Holy Spirit is sent out. No matter where a person may be, as long as his spirit is open to God and desires God, the Holy Spirit will visit Him by "looking at him." God's visiting us by looking at us is the way in which He cares for us. This is carried out through the Holy Spirit and is the work of the Holy Spirit. The Holy Spirit is the eyes of the Lamb, which are sent forth into all the earth to look at those who are on the earth.

THE HOLY SPIRIT CAUSING MAN TO BE REGENERATED
AND TO HAVE THE LIFE OF GOD

When the Holy Spirit looks at a person, the lamps of the fire of God shine upon him, and when the lamps of fire shine upon him, the consuming fire of God burns within him. This consuming fire is both God Himself and the Spirit, because God Himself is both a consuming fire and the Spirit. Through this looking, shining, and burning, God who is in Christ, and Christ who is in the Holy Spirit are wrought into us. As a result, we receive the element of the Holy Spirit, the element of Christ, and the element of God. From that time on we have the element of God in addition to our human element. God is added into us. We are like a cup, and as such we are able to contain the Spirit of God, the fire of God, the life of God, and the nature of God. This is the way in which those who are saved have the element of God within them.

THE HOLY SPIRIT CAUSING MAN
TO BE TRANSFORMED IN HIS SOUL

From the day that we are regenerated onward, God not only lives within us but also moves and works within us in many ways in order to bring our soul and body into God. The

Holy Spirit who dwells in us will eventually bring every part of our soul—our mind, emotion, and will—into the Spirit.

When our mind, emotion, and will are gradually, step by step, brought into the Spirit, they will become the spiritual mind, the spiritual emotion, and the spiritual will. When this happens, we will become spiritual people. Today we are saved, and God who is the Spirit is in us. However, even though the Spirit is in us, our living may not be in the Spirit. Our mind, emotion, and will may not have entered the Spirit, may not submit to the ruling of the Spirit, and may not be directed by the Spirit. Our mind still may be the master, thinking whatever it pleases; our emotion still may be free to love and hate whatever it feels to; and, even more, our will still may be independent, choosing and determining as it wills. Although we have a spirit, and the Spirit of God is also in us, we may be living entirely by our soul—we may still make decisions and love, hate, and think by ourselves. We still may not care for the existence of our spirit or submit to the ruling of the Spirit of God. Hence, even though we are saved, we still may be soulish, fleshly, and of the self. In short, we still may not be spiritual.

A PROPER CHRISTIAN BEING ONE WHO IS IN SPIRIT

The situation of a normal Christian should be that he is one who lives in the Spirit. His mind, emotion, and will should submit to the ruling of the Spirit and be directed by the Spirit. When the Spirit directs him to think a certain way, he should think that way; when the spirit directs him to love in a particular way, he should love in that way; and when the Spirit directs him to make a certain decision, he should make that decision. Such a person is not lacking a mind, emotion, or will. In fact, he has a strong mind, emotion, and will, yet his mind, emotion, and will are no longer in the first place but in the second place. They entirely submit to the ruling of the Spirit, allowing the Spirit to have the preeminence and be the Lord. His mind, his preferences, his opinions, and his decisions are ruled and directed by the Spirit, and as a result, he is spiritual. This kind of Christian living is the normal Christian living. In this kind of living not only does God enter into man, but man is also brought into God by the Spirit of God. A person who lives this way not only has God in him but is also in God.

TURNING TO THE SPIRIT
TO BE DIRECTED BY THE SPIRIT

After we were regenerated and saved, God entered into us. But the question remains, have we also entered into God? If we have entered into God, we will live in God. God has entered into us, but have we also entered into God? Have our mind, emotion, will, preferences, and opinions entered into God? Is our living under the ruling of the Holy Spirit and directed by God? This is a very serious matter. I am afraid that we still may not have entered into God. Our mind, emotion, and will are still independent of God, we still have not submitted to the Holy Spirit, and we still have not entered into the Holy Spirit. Although God is in us, we do not live in God and are still independent.

We should never take this speaking as a doctrine. If we check with ourselves based on this word, we may find that the inner condition of our mind, emotion, and will are truly independent of God. Even though we may pray and ask the Lord for His forgiveness, sometimes when faced with a situation, we still may secretly resolve in our heart that we will fellowship with the Lord only after first considering the matter on our own. Do not think that this is a joke. This truly may be our situation. It may be that only after we deem that we have adequately thought about a particular matter on our own, and only after we have taken what we deem to be the necessary actions on our own, do we come back to the Lord to seek Him.

THE EMOTION BEING MADE SPIRITUAL

This is the case not only with our mind and will but also with our emotion. Many times, the love even among the brothers is soulish, emotional, and fleshly, and the love among the sisters is entirely outside of the Holy Spirit and is not controlled or ruled by the Holy Spirit. For example, it is often the case that one sister really likes another sister and spends much time with her to shop, chat, and joke. Although the Holy Spirit gives this sister the feeling that she is too much and is improper, she ignores this feeling and considers that it is not important. She simply continues to act according to her own will. From this we can see that many times the more the Holy Spirit prohibits us, the more independent our emotion becomes. This is because we are still living in our soul—sometimes we live in our mind, sometimes we live in our emotion, and sometimes we live in our will. For us to live in God, we need death and resurrection, which will allow the Spirit of God to bring every single part of our being into God, so that we may submit to the ruling and direction of the Spirit.

THE WILL BEING MADE SPIRITUAL

Philippians 2:13 says, "For it is God who operates in you both the willing and the working for His good pleasure." This means that outwardly there is a working, inwardly there is a willing, and both this willing and working are God's operation in us. God operates in us in this way because it is His purpose that our will be brought under His ruling. Thus, we must experience God's operating in us. God is in us, and His intention is to bring our willing and working under His ruling. For this, He operates in us to rule our willing and working so that we will no longer rely on ourselves.

As those who have been saved, we have God in us, but often our willing and working are not under God's ruling, the ruling of the Holy Spirit. Sometimes we decide to be ruled by the Holy Spirit, but other times we allow our will to be independent. Our willing has not submitted to and is not under the direction of the operation of God. This is even more the case with our outward working. If we want to go east, we go east, and if we want to go west, we go west. Whatever we want to do, we do it. Although outwardly this may not result in any big mistakes, the most obvious and greatest mistake is that we are not directed by the operation of the Holy Spirit while we do these things. While the Spirit is operating in His way, we continue to work in our own way. Sometimes we even press the Holy Spirit to the extent that He does not operate in us anymore. Because we ignore Him when He operates in us, eventually He stops operating in us.

Philippians 2 reveals that God wants to work in us to the point where both our inward willing and outward working are brought under the Holy Spirit and are directed by the operation of the Holy Spirit. If both our willing and working are under the operation of God, we will be brought into God and will spontaneously enter into the Spirit. When we are brought to this point, although we continue to have outward workings and continue to work, our working is no longer something of ourselves but of God and of the Spirit within us. When the Spirit within us moves in a particular way, we will work in that way, and when the Spirit within us moves in another way, we will work in that way. Our outward activities will come from the operating and moving of the Spirit of God in our spirit, and our entire being will be under the Spirit of God. When we are in submission to the Spirit of God, we will have spiritual reality, and when we are under the Spirit of God, spiritual reality will be expressed through us.

THE MIND BEING MADE SPIRITUAL

Romans 8 tells us that our mind may be set either on the flesh or on the spirit (v. 6). If our mind is set on the flesh, our mind will become the mind of the flesh, and if our mind is set on the spirit, our mind will become the mind of the spirit. The will of God is to bring our mind under the ruling of the Spirit so that our mind will become a mind of the spirit, a spiritual mind. When our mind has become a spiritual mind, then our thoughts will be the result of the ruling and direction of the Holy Spirit and not the issue of our independent mind. At this point, our mind will be in God and of God.

LIVING IN THE SPIRIT
TO LIVE OUT SPIRITUAL REALITY

Our mind, emotion, and will should be under the ruling of the Holy Spirit. Whether we are loving the brothers or fellowshipping with the sisters, all of our emotions should be restricted and ruled by the Holy Spirit. If the Holy Spirit agrees with our love, then we should love, but if the Holy

Spirit is against our love, then we should not love. Our love must be under the ruling of the Holy Spirit. Similarly, our mind has to submit to the leading of the Holy Spirit, and our will has to follow the feeling of the Holy Spirit. In this way, every part of our soul—our mind, emotion, and will—may be brought into God. At this time we will be those who live in God and in the Spirit, and our living will have spiritual reality.

The Holy Spirit's blessing and working in us are to bring us into God so that our entire being—our mind, emotion, and will—will be brought into God and directed and ruled by the Spirit. Then the Spirit of God will not only be in us but will also dwell in us and regulate everything within us. In this way we will no longer be soulish or fleshly but spiritual, and we will have the expression of a spiritual condition. This will be spiritual reality.

CHAPTER SIX

EXPERIENCING SPIRITUAL REALITY IN THE HOLY SPIRIT

John 16:13 says, "But when He, the Spirit of reality, comes, He will guide you into all the reality." This verse does not speak merely of understanding the truth but of being guided by the Spirit of reality into all the reality.

INCARNATION

God has a purpose in this universe, and this purpose is to mingle Himself with man to the extent that man would be exactly the same as He is. God is Spirit—His essence, nature, and being are Spirit. Thus, for Him to mingle with man, man must have a spirit that is identical to and compatible with the essence of God. Only in this way can God's Spirit be mingled with the human spirit, interact with the human spirit, and be joined with the human spirit as one spirit. For God to enter into man, mingle with man, and make man exactly the same as He is, He first had to become flesh. The Lord Jesus' becoming flesh was His coming by the Spirit into man (cf. Matt. 1:20). Becoming flesh was the first step that the Lord Jesus had to take.

DEATH, RESURRECTION, AND ASCENSION

After becoming flesh, the further steps that the incarnated Lord Jesus took were to die, resurrect, and ascend to the heavens. The Lord's death dealt with all the problems in the universe between God and man. Man's sin, the world, Satan, the flesh, man's corruption, and man's opposition toward God have all been dealt with and terminated by the death of the Lord Jesus. This is the significance of His death.

The significance of His resurrection is that it enables man
to receive everything of God, that is, it brings man into all
the riches of God. On the negative side, death solves all the
problems between God and man, and on the positive side, resurrection brings man into the riches of God.

In addition to dying and resurrecting, the Lord Jesus
also ascended to the heavens. He entered into and attained
to the heavenly nature and the heavenly blessings. When
He ascended, this God who is Spirit was no longer merely
God or merely Spirit, because by that time He had already
passed through incarnation, death, and resurrection. Before
incarnation, our God was in the heavens. At that time He was
purely God, purely Spirit, and there was nothing other than
the element of God and Spirit in Him and on Him. He was
God, and He was Spirit. This was His situation before His
incarnation.

BECOMING THE HOLY SPIRIT AND DESCENDING
ON THE DAY OF PENTECOST

One day God came down from the heavens and entered
into man to become flesh. God's becoming flesh was God's
putting on of man—His putting on of the element and nature
of man. However, God did not stop there. He not only became
flesh but also passed through death and resurrection. When
He became flesh, the element of humanity was added into
Him; when He passed through death, the element and power
of death was added into Him; when He passed through resurrection, the element of resurrection was added into Him; and
when He ascended to the heavens, the element of ascension
was added into Him. Thus, today God is not the same as He
was before incarnation. He is not merely God or merely Spirit.
Now He has more elements—the elements of incarnation,
death, resurrection, and ascension are all in Him.

ALL THE FULLNESS OF GOD BEING
IN THE HOLY SPIRIT

After becoming flesh, dying, resurrecting, and ascending, God descended on the day of Pentecost. The One who
descended was the Holy Spirit; however, the Holy Spirit who

descended was not the God before incarnation but the God who possessed additional elements to those He originally possessed. When He descended on the day of Pentecost, He had already passed through incarnation, death, resurrection, and ascension. When He descended, He was surely God, but in addition to possessing the element of God, He also possessed the element of man because He had become flesh. Moreover, He not only possessed the element of man as a result of becoming flesh, He also had the elements of death, resurrection, and ascension within Him as a result of dying, resurrecting, and ascending. Hence, the Holy Spirit who descended from heaven on the day of Pentecost was very rich. Within Him there was God, man, death, resurrection, and ascension. We can also say that this Spirit possessed the death of the cross, the life of resurrection, and the riches of ascension.

The Christ who died, resurrected, and ascended descended as the Holy Spirit on the day of Pentecost, and all that God is and has, as well as all that He had done, had passed through, had accomplished, and had attained to were in Him. God Himself and the humanity that God had put on were in Him. The death of the cross and its effectiveness were in Him. The power of resurrection and its effectiveness were in Him. The ascension of Christ with its reality, content, and authority were also all in Him. God and all that He has passed through were in the Holy Spirit on the day of Pentecost and continue to be in Him today.

After we are saved, the Holy Spirit lives within us, but very few of us realize how rich this Holy Spirit who dwells in us is. Not only is God in the Holy Spirit, but the humanity of the God who was incarnated is also in the Holy Spirit. Moreover, the death of the cross, resurrection, ascension, and the riches and authority of the heavens are in the Holy Spirit. Therefore, when the Holy Spirit comes into us, He comes into us with all His riches.

God is the Spirit, and the Spirit is God Himself, but when God became flesh, He passed through man and put on humanity. From that day on, God had no way to put off His humanity. *Hymns,* #132 says that today in heaven God still has humanity. Today our Savior God still has humanity in heaven (Acts 7:56).

How do we know this? We know this because He passed through humanity and put on humanity, and after His death and resurrection, He entered into ascension with this humanity (Mark 16:19; Luke 24:51; Acts 2:32-33).

Today the Holy Spirit has the element of God, the element of man, the element of death, the element of resurrection, the element of ascension, and the element of the riches of the heavens in Him. This is the Holy Spirit who is in us. Although we are so small and He is so great and so rich, the Holy Spirit is within us.

Before God entered into us, He passed through incarnation in Bethlehem and crucifixion on Golgotha. He also passed through burial in the tomb, resurrection, and even ascension, in which He received all the authority in heaven and on earth (Matt. 28:18). After passing through all these processes, God as the Spirit descended and entered into us. The riches of all that God is and has done are in this Spirit.

THE HOLY SPIRIT BEING
THE ANSWER TO EVERY QUESTION

It may be the case that we are often touched by the Lord's great love that was manifested in His redemption. We may vividly and genuinely see the Lord's death and His great love. Thus, when we think of Him, we may often be touched to the point of shedding tears. However, when we come to preach the gospel, we may not know how to present to people this love of the Lord Jesus that He displayed on the cross and in His precious, cleansing blood. Today, however, we have found the secret. We have seen that the Holy Spirit is able to show man the precious blood of the cross just like the scene on a television screen is shown and that in doing so the Holy Spirit is not constrained by time or space. The great love displayed on the cross and the precious, redeeming blood are in the Holy Spirit. If we know the mystery that everything is in the Spirit, we will realize that all the questions that we do not know how to answer can be answered by the Holy Spirit.

ALL SPIRITUAL REALITY BEING IN THE HOLY SPIRIT

For example, when we preach the gospel to people, we may

tell them that Jesus died for them on the cross and shed His precious blood for them. However, if they ask, "Where is the cross? Where is this precious blood?" we are not able to show them these things. Although we are not able to show them, as we are speaking to them, the Holy Spirit creates an image in their spirit, showing them the scene of the Lord on the cross so that they not only hear the truth of the gospel but also see a spiritual vision of what they are hearing. This spiritual vision is spiritual reality. The cross, resurrection, ascension, and all that God is and has done are in the Holy Spirit. All spiritual reality is in the Holy Spirit.

The Holy Spirit brings God Himself, incarnation, redemption, the shedding of blood, the substitutionary death, resurrection, ascension, glory, authority, and the throne to man. After passing through all these processes, God became the Spirit of reality. All spiritual reality is in the Holy Spirit. In ourselves, our ability to experience spiritual reality is limited by time and space, but time and space do not exist in the Holy Spirit, and He has brought all these realities directly into us. In the past all these realities were not available to us. But today the shedding of the precious blood, resurrection, ascension, and all these realities are in the Holy Spirit, and the Holy Spirit has brought all these realities into us.

In John 14 the Lord said that when He went away, He would send the Holy Spirit. What does the Holy Spirit do when He comes? When He comes, the Holy Spirit guides us into all the reality. When we tell people that there is God, they may ask, "Where is God?" To man, God is not real. But we have to remember that in the Holy Spirit God is real. When a person touches the Holy Spirit, the Holy Spirit brings him into the reality where he is able to touch God. When we tell people that Jesus was crucified, this is merely a doctrine to them. To them, the cross is not real. But in the Holy Spirit the cross becomes real, and in the Holy Spirit man can touch and experience the cross. In the same principle, when we tell the children of God that they are of Christ and that they have been resurrected with Christ, this may be vague to them. When they touch the Holy Spirit, however, this spiritual reality will be in them, and resurrection will become real to them.

THE HOLY SPIRIT BEING THE SPIRIT OF REALITY

All spiritual reality is in the Holy Spirit, so the Holy Spirit is the Spirit of reality. In the Holy Spirit, the Spirit of reality, God is real. In addition, incarnation, the cross, resurrection, ascension, the throne, authority, blessing, and the glory in the heavens are all real. If all these things were not in the Holy Spirit, there would be no spiritual reality. This is why many unbelievers ask: "Is there God in this universe?" "Is there the cross?" "Is there resurrection?" "Is there ascension?" Although there is truly a spiritual reality of all these matters, for finite man all of these matters are too far away. To those who believe in God, however, these things are very close, even intimately close, because all these things are in the Holy Spirit, and the Holy Spirit is in those who believe. Whenever we touch the Holy Spirit, all these matters become real to us, because all these matters are real in the Holy Spirit. Whenever we touch the Holy Spirit, we touch death, resurrection, ascension, and the throne. To those who have never touched the Holy Spirit, all these things seem not to exist.

SPIRITUAL REALITY NOT BEING
PRODUCED BY IMITATION

The reality of everything that we believe is in the Holy Spirit. What we believe does not come to us through teaching, rebuking, exhortation, copying, or imitation. Any living that is the result of imitation is not a genuine Christian living. The genuine Christian living does not come from imitation or teaching but from the Spirit. In the past, there was a brother from Germany named George Müller. This brother knew how to come near to God and receive the leading of the Spirit in his spirit. He was one who had many experiences of faith. As a result, many Christians from the past imitated him, and even today many continue to do so. However, none of those who have tried merely to imitate him have learned to do so successfully, because spirituality does not come from learning or imitation. Spiritual reality depends on the human spirit touching the Spirit of God. Because spiritual reality is in the Holy Spirit, in order for a person to have it, his human spirit has to touch the Holy Spirit.

NORMAL CHRISTIAN LIVING BEING
A MATTER OF TURNING TO THE SPIRIT

Teachings in themselves do not have reality. Thus, being a Christian does not depend on teachings. Spiritual reality depends on the Holy Spirit, and today this exceedingly rich Spirit is dwelling in our spirit. As long as we turn to our spirit, we will touch the Spirit who is God Himself and who contains all spiritual riches and reality. If we learn to reject our emotion, desires, inclinations, views, thoughts, and opinions, putting them in a secondary position, and learn to turn to our spirit, we will touch the Spirit, and we will touch God. Eventually, this Spirit will be to us the reality of whatever we need. When we need shining, we will receive shining, when we need guidance, we will receive guidance, and when we need resurrection power, we will receive resurrection power. The Spirit today is all-sufficient and surpassingly rich. Everything of God, including all that He has accomplished, passed through, and attained, is now in the Holy Spirit, and the Holy Spirit has already entered into our spirit.

The secret to having a normal Christian living is to deny our mind, our emotion, and our will, putting everything we have in second place, and to turn to our spirit, the deepest part of our being. Our inmost part is our spirit, and the One who dwells in our spirit is the Holy Spirit. All spiritual riches and reality are in the Holy Spirit. Thus, genuine Christian living is not a matter of how much teaching we have heard or understood or of how much resolution and determination we have; genuine Christian living is a matter of living in our spirit. There is only one basic lesson to learn for our Christian living—to turn to our spirit. As long as we turn to our spirit, our mind, emotion, and will spontaneously are put in second place, and our spirit will have the first place. Then we will be able to contact and touch the Spirit of God in our spirit that we may touch the reality of the Holy Spirit. All the spiritual reality that we need can be received by us in this Spirit because all spiritual reality is in the Holy Spirit.

CHAPTER SEVEN

THE SPIRIT FOR LIVING

THE CHRISTIAN LIVING BEING A LIFE OF MAN BEING MINGLED WITH GOD

A Christian is one who has God mingled with him. Hence, the normal Christian living is not a living that is independent or outside of God. It is a living that submits to the ruling of God, is under the direction of God, and is mingled with God.

How can man live a life that is mingled with God? God is Spirit, and when we are saved, God as the Spirit enters into our spirit, interacts with our spirit, and is joined to our spirit as one spirit. Hence, whenever we turn to our spirit and are in our spirit, we meet Him because He has been mingled with our spirit to become one spirit. When we turn to our spirit, we actually turn to Him as the Spirit. Our entire Christian living should be one that is lived out from the spirit. In our Christian living, the question is not whether we should or should not do certain things. Rather, the question is whether we do them from our soul or from our spirit.

NOT BEING A QUESTION OF WHAT WE DO BUT OF HOW WE DO IT

The center of the Christian living is not a matter of doing the right thing but a matter of who is doing it. It is not a matter of what we do but a matter of who is doing it. In other words, is it our soul that does things or our spirit? Do we do things in our soul, or does God do them in our spirit? Our Christian living is not a matter of what to do but of how to do things. Is it our soul that does things, or is it our spirit? Almost every Christian who desires to learn to live before the Lord prays, "Lord, what is the right thing for me to do? What is pleasing to You for me to do?" The fact is that this kind of prayer does not match the spiritual reality because the key is not what we do but whether or not we have God in what we do. Is God doing a certain thing with us, or are we doing it by ourselves? Are we doing it by being mingled with God, or are we doing it on our own? Are we doing it from our soul, or are we doing it from our spirit? If we do something from our soul, we are doing it on our own, but if we do something from our spirit, we are doing it by being mingled with God.

For example, if a certain locality invites you to go to their meeting, you should kneel down before the Lord and say, "O Lord, are You going?" Please note that you should not ask, "O Lord, do You want me to go? Should I go?" Rather, you should say, "O Lord, if You go, I will follow You. If You go, You have to go by putting me on." Suppose you had a suit that could speak. If you were about to go to the meeting, it would bother you, saying, "Are you going to the meeting?" You would say, "Yes, I am going." Then the suit would say, "Please put me on." Then you would put the suit on. Thus, when you move, the suit moves. When you stand, the suit stands, and when you bend, the suit bends. The suit is "mingled" with you, and you are moving with the suit. Hence, wherever we go and whatever we do, if we do not have the inward assurance that it is the Lord who is going to a certain place or doing a certain thing by putting us on, then we know that we should not go there or do that thing. We should not ask the Lord whether or not we should do a particular thing but whether or not He is doing it.

THE TURNING POINT OF THE CHRISTIAN LIFE

In the church life we find that there are some people who attend every meeting, who pray in every meeting, and who pray long prayers every time they pray. But the strange thing is that year after year they do not appear to make any spiritual turns or spiritual progress. This is because they still take themselves as the center in their living and do not pay attention to the sense in their spirit. They work by themselves and do not allow the Spirit to work. This should be a warning to us. Every time before we go to a meeting, we first must ask the Lord, "O Lord, are You going to the meeting? Are You going to the meeting with me? Lord, are You wearing me to the meeting? If so, I will go with You." Then when we get to the meeting, we do not need to consider whether or not we should pray or how we should pray. Rather, we should ask the Lord silently, "O Lord, do You want to pray? Are You putting me on to pray? If so, I will pray with You." Outwardly it may seem that we are the ones who are praying, but actually we are cooperating with the Lord in prayer.

Our entire living, not just our prayer, should be like this. Consider loving the brothers for example. We should not ask the Lord whether or not we should love a certain brother. Rather, we should ask, "O Lord, do You love this brother? Will You put me on to love him? Will You love Him with me?" We must hold tightly to this principle—the principle of not asking what to do but how to do it. Do we do things independently, or does the Lord wear us to do them? Do we do things from our soul, or do we do them from our spirit? It is wrong to teach people to pay attention to what they should or should not do. What we need to ask constantly is, "O Lord, this matter may be right, but are You doing it? Are You wearing me to do this? Are You doing this with me? O Lord, are You in me while I am doing this? Are You doing this with me?" If this were the situation, our Christian life would have a great turn.

NOT A MATTER OF DOING GOOD OR EVIL
BUT A MATTER OF DOING EVERYTHING IN SPIRIT

Romans 7 and 8 are two chapters in the Bible that are completely different from each other. The focus of chapter seven is altogether different from that of chapter eight; thus, the central points of these two chapters are also different. The central point of chapter seven is that the "I" wants to do good and does not want to do evil. What it speaks of is related to the matter of good and evil, and what it focuses on is whether the "I" does good or evil. This is Romans 7. When we come to chapter eight, it is altogether not a matter of good and evil. In chapter eight there is only spirit and life. Chapter eight does not speak of the "I" doing good. Rather, it says that we should no longer live in the flesh but in the spirit. Chapter eight does not speak of doing good or doing evil. Rather, it is concerned with whether we do things in the flesh or in the spirit.

This shows us that Romans 7 and 8 are absolutely different. In chapter seven it is a matter of good or evil, that is, a matter of what we do. But in chapter eight it is a matter of the flesh or the spirit, that is, a matter of who does it. Chapter seven focuses on what we do—good or evil, whereas chapter eight focuses on who does it—the flesh or the spirit. Do not say that only what is evil is wrong. In God's eyes even what is good may be wrong. Only what is done by the spirit is right.

For example, suppose there is a sister who, after waking up in the morning, becomes irritated by her child because he does not listen to her. At that time what is the right thing for her to do—to pray or to get angry? Of course, we all would say that she should pray, because it is right to pray and wrong to get angry. However, does the problem end there? Would it be enough for our sister to no longer be angry and to kneel down to pray? Suppose that when she kneels down to pray, she truly thanks and praises the Lord that although she should have been angry, she is not and instead is praying. Most people would say that this sister is very good. I am afraid that even we would testify for her, saying how good she is because she has such a good testimony. She should have been angry, but instead she asked the Lord, "Should I be angry, or should I pray?" In the end she prayed, so we would praise her. However, please remember that this matter does not end there. We have to ask a further question: When she knelt down to pray, was she the one praying, or was it the Lord who was praying? Did she put up with her child by herself and force herself to pray, or was the Lord praying with her? These two situations are completely different and are very serious.

LIVING IN THE LORD AND BEING MINGLED
WITH THE SPIRIT OF THE LORD

Many times when we kneel down to pray, we are the ones who are praying. In other words, the Lord is not with us in our prayer. When the sister with the disobedient child kneels down to pray in the morning, she may say, "O Lord, You see that this child is very disobedient, and I should have beaten him, but I did not beat him. Rather, I came to pray and tell You this matter." While she is saying this, however, within her there may be a voice saying, "O Lord, look how disobedient this sister is." While she is bringing her accusations concerning the child's disobedience to the Lord, deep within her there may be another voice accusing her, saying, "You are also disobedient." She may persist, saying, "O Lord, I told him three or four times to obey, but he still did not listen to me." Then the Lord may say in her, "You are just the same. I have told you to obey three or four times, yet you still do not listen to me." Hence, this kind of prayer may be the sister's praying in herself, not the Lord's putting her on to pray or the Lord's mingling with her in prayer.

Then what kind of prayer is the Lord's prayer in us? Many times we are the same as that sister. When we pray, it is often the faculties of our soul—our mind, emotion, and will—that pray. We often pray according to our resolution, thought, emotion, and preference. At these times, however, the Spirit of God, the Lord Himself, will often give us the feeling in our spirit that our children's disobedience is to remind us that we are also disobedient before the Lord. We may start by praying before the Lord concerning our children, but gradually, we will bring our own situation before Him and pray for ourselves.

Here we see that there are two layers. On the superficial layer we may pray concerning our children. This is the activity of our soul. On the deeper layer, however, we may have a feeling in our spirit that our situation is not good and that we need to pray for ourselves. If we do not care for this feeling in our spirit but merely pray according to the activity of our soul, saying, "O Lord, this child is disobedient," the Lord within us will not pray with us. Instead, He will condemn and enlighten us inwardly. If we have learned the spiritual lesson, we would cease immediately, turn to our spirit, follow the feeling in our spirit, speak with the Lord, and move with the

Lord. We would open our mouth and say, "O Lord, I have not listened to You for a long time. I am a rebellious one. Even though You told me to obey three or four times, I still did not listen to You. Lord, forgive me." At such a time, are we praying from our soul or from our spirit? We are praying from our spirit. Is it we who are praying or is it the Lord who is praying? It is the Lord putting us on to pray. It is the Lord praying in coordination with us and we praying in coordination with the Lord.

If we do not pray like this, we will pray from the soul according to our preferences, decisions, and ideas. Sometimes we may even pray to a point where we cry, "O Lord, I really do not know how to deal with this child." The wonderful thing is that it is at this time that we have another feeling deep within us that we truly do not have any way. Therefore, we have to see that there are two layers in our prayer. We may pray on the superficial layer or on the deeper layer. Do not merely ask whether it is right to be angry or to pray. To know this is insufficient. We must ask ourselves further whether it is we who pray or the Lord putting us on to pray and whether it is our soul or our spirit praying.

Hence, in our Christian living we should not merely ask what to do but how to do a certain thing. We must ask who is doing it—the flesh or the spirit? Are we doing it by the soul or by the spirit? Are we doing it, or is the Lord who puts us on doing it? The Christian living is not a living outside of the Lord, that is, a living in which we reject evil and do good by ourselves. This is merely the living of a Gentile or of a good man. The Christian living is a living that is in the Lord and is mingled with the Spirit of the Lord. This kind of living is one that also rejects evil and does good, but in this kind of living we do not do these things by ourselves. Rather, we are mingled with the Lord, and we do these things with the Lord. It is the Lord doing them by putting us on and by being mingled with us. Our living should not be merely a good living but a living that is the mingling of God and man. This is a living that is God mingled with man and man mingled with God, the two being mingled together. This is the Christian living.

Hence, in our Christian living we should not merely ask

whether or not it is right to do something. Rather, we should ask who is doing it. Only when we are in the mingled spirit, in which God mingles with man and man mingles with God, and only in such a spirit of living can we have the proper Christian living and service.

CHAPTER EIGHT

THE RELATIONSHIP
BETWEEN SPIRIT AND LIFE

THE SPIRIT GIVING LIFE

In John 6:63 the Lord said, "It is the Spirit who gives life; the flesh profits nothing; the words which I have spoken to you are spirit and are life." Both *spirit* and *life* are mentioned twice in this verse. In the first instance, *the Spirit* and *life* are connected together in the phrase, "It is the Spirit who gives life." In the second instance, *spirit* and *life* are separated in the phrase, "The words which I have spoken to you are spirit and are life." The Lord's words are spirit and are life. Romans 8:2 mentions "the law of the Spirit of life." The Spirit is the Spirit of life, and this law is of the Spirit. Thus, it is the law of the Spirit of life. Verse 6 says, "For the mind set on the flesh is death, but the mind set on the spirit is life and peace." Whenever we set our mind on the spirit, we have life and peace. Second Corinthians 3:6 states, "The letter kills, but the Spirit gives life." This matches what is said in John 6:63.

GOD BEING JOINED TO
AND MINGLED WITH MAN IN SPIRIT

The Bible says that God is Spirit (4:24). However, as far as God's relationship with man is concerned, we may say that God in eternity, before entering into time, was purely God, but when this God reaches man, what man touches is the Spirit. This means that when God is in His dwelling place, He is God, but when He comes out of His heavenly sanctuary and works on the earth to contact man, He is the Spirit who can be touched by man. In other words, God in Himself is God, but whenever He comes out of Himself to the earth to work, to

contact man, and even to enter into man, what man touches
is the Spirit. Hence, God being Spirit has two implications.
On the one hand, He is God, and on the other hand, He is the
Spirit. When He is in His sanctuary, He is God, but when He
comes out of His sanctuary, comes into the midst of men, and
enters into men, He is the Spirit. As the Spirit He mingles
with and joins with man to be one. In a sense, it is not God
who mingles with and joins with man as one, but it is the
Spirit who mingles with man as one. As the Spirit God is
joined with man's spirit to be one spirit. Thus, God's relationship with man is altogether a matter of the spirit. Therefore,
the experience, living, and work of a Christian should be
in the spirit.

MAN LIVING AND WORKING IN SPIRIT

We all know that the first experience of a Christian is salvation through regeneration. Regeneration is a matter of the
spirit. The first time God touches man, and the first time
man contacts God, man is regenerated in his spirit. Man's
being regenerated in his spirit is the first step of his having a
relationship with God. In this first step man touches God in
the Spirit of God, and the Spirit of God joins with man in the
spirit of man. In other words, the God who is Spirit enters
into the spirit of man and is joined to man. This is regeneration.
After our regeneration, we need to have spiritual experiences,
make spiritual progress, live a spiritual living, and do spiritual work. All of these must be in our spirit. This spirit is the
Spirit of God fellowshipping with our spirit, being joined to
our spirit, and being mingled with our spirit as one spirit. In
regeneration the Spirit of God and our spirit become one
spirit and therefore inseparable. Thus, our Christian living
and work should be in this spirit.

Any time we do not live in such a spirit, regardless of
whether we are right or wrong, we are not living a normal
Christian life. The normal Christian life is not a matter of
right and wrong but a matter of whether or not we are in the
spirit. It is not that to rise up in the morning and then to lose
our temper is wrong but to pray is right, or that to rise up in
the morning and then to be angry with people is wrong but to

have morning watch is right. What matters is whether our morning watch, reading the Bible, and praying are in the spirit or outside of the spirit. If our morning watch, praying, and reading of the Bible are in the spirit, then this is the normal Christian life. But if they are outside of the spirit, we are living a religious life, not a normal Christian life.

Some people may ask what the distinction between a Christian and a religious person is. In brief, a Christian is one who lives in the spirit whereas a religious person does not live in the spirit but in a kind of religious ritual. For instance, suppose you are a Christian, but you do not live in your spirit. Rather, you strictly observe religious regulations, read the Bible, and pray daily, living a life of Christian rituals. This is a religious living. Just because you read the Bible, pray, speak the truth to people, and attend services every Lord's Day does not mean that you are living a Christian life. Many times our reading the Bible, praying, talking about the truth, or even preaching the truth are nothing but aspects of a religious living, not a living in the spirit. This is because our reading of the Bible, praying, speaking, and preaching of the truth are often outside of the spirit and are not in the spirit.

LIVING IN THE SPIRIT
BEING TO LIVE IN RESURRECTION

I hope that every Christian would be clear that the relationship God desires to have with us is a relationship in which He as the Spirit enters into our spirit and in which we saved ones live in this spirit. When we live in the spirit, we are living in resurrection. When we live in resurrection, we experience dying with Christ and ascending with Christ. In other words, when we live in the spirit, we live in the realm of resurrection, and the death of the cross has an effect on us. This death enables us to put off everything that is incompatible with God so that we may live in the heavenlies. At this time, the heavenly condition is manifested in us. In such a spirit, we can sense that we are heavenly people.

GOD, SPIRIT, RESURRECTION, DEATH, AND ASCENSION

Hence, we see that there are five things that are linked

together: first, God being Spirit; second, living in the Spirit; third, living in resurrection; fourth, experiencing the death of the cross; and fifth, experiencing ascension. In short, God is Spirit, and to live in the Spirit is to live in resurrection. Living in resurrection leads us to the experience of death on the one hand and the experience of ascension on the other. These five items are linked together. God is Spirit, so God is the first item, and the Spirit is the second item. To live in the Spirit is to live in resurrection, so resurrection is the third item. One who lives in resurrection will have the experience of death and ascension, so death is the fourth item, and ascension is the fifth item. These five items—God, Spirit, resurrection, death, and ascension—are linked to us.

In our spiritual experience, when we live in our spirit we sense the presence of the Lord as a kind of transcendency. On the one hand, we experience death, which is a suffering to us, but on the other hand, we are brought into a heavenly realm, into a kind of spiritual reality, where we transcend over all hardship and suffering. This indicates that to live in the spirit is to live in a realm, a sphere, where there is God, the presence of God, the experience of death, and the experience of ascension. In other words, when we live in our spirit, we live in resurrection, and when we live in resurrection, we touch spiritual reality. In this spiritual reality we have the presence of God and the experience of death on the one hand and the experience of ascension on the other. Any time we turn to live in our spirit, we are living in resurrection, and at that time we sense the presence of the Lord. On the one hand, we experience death, which delivers us from all persons, things, and matters that are contrary to God, and on the other hand, we experience ascension, which gives us the sense that we are in the heavenly sphere. Not only God is with us, but heaven is also with us.

THE RELATIONSHIP BETWEEN SPIRIT AND LIFE

We have already seen these five great matters—God, God being Spirit, living in the Spirit being to live in resurrection, and living in resurrection causing us to have the experiences of death and ascension. However, we have not seen how these things are related to life, nor have we seen the matter of life. Whether we are speaking of the Spirit, resurrection, death, or ascension, the source is God. God is Spirit, and when the Spirit comes out and enters into us, we live in Him and experience resurrection. This resurrection brings with it death and ascension. All of these matters are related to life and cannot be separated from life.

What is the relationship between the Spirit and life, and how are they distinct? We all know that the Holy Spirit gives life that man may have life, yet we may not be clear about the difference between the Holy Spirit and life and between life and the Holy Spirit. For example, we all know that God is Spirit, and we also know the definitions of the Spirit and of God and their distinctions. Now we have to know what the Lord Jesus said concerning the Spirit. He said that it is the Spirit who gives life and that the words which He spoke are spirit and life (John 6:63). Obviously, life is connected to the Holy Spirit. Moreover, the Spirit of life, which is spoken of in Romans 8:2, is also referred to as the Spirit who gives life (v. 11). Romans 8 says that to touch the Spirit is to touch life and that the mind set on the spirit is life and peace (v. 6). These verses show us that the Bible links life and the Holy Spirit together.

We saved ones, in speaking about the Spirit and life, may often say things like, "This brother is quite good in life," or, "This sister is very strong in the spiritual life." Actually, this is the speaking of an unlearned person. Life does not carry distinctions such as good or bad, strong or weak. Everything of life is good and beautiful; it is never bad or wrong. Everything of life is strong. Only death is not strong.

What is life? What is the relationship between life and the Spirit, and what distinguishes them from each other? Psalm 36 reads, "For with You is the fountain of life" (v. 9). The Lord is the fountain of life, and this fountain of life is in God. When the Lord Jesus came to the earth, John declared at the very beginning of the Gospel of John, "In Him was life, and the life was the light of men" (1:4). From this we see that life was in the Lord Jesus. In addition to this, the Lord Himself said, "I am the resurrection and the life" (11:25). The Lord is life, and life is in Him. Then in chapter six He said that it is the Spirit who gives life, and the words which He spoke are spirit and are life. In the age of the apostles, Paul said that the Spirit is the Spirit of life (Rom. 8:2). In Romans 8 he said that by setting our mind on the spirit we touch life and that the mind set on the spirit is life (v. 6). In 1 John 5 the apostle John even said, "He who has the Son has the life; he who does not have the Son of God does not have the life" (v. 12). If we combine all these verses together, we can see that life is the Lord Himself.

THE DISTINCTION BETWEEN GOD AND SPIRIT

We all know that God is the Spirit, that the Spirit is God, and that there is no difference between the Spirit and God. But as far as God's relationship with man is concerned, there is a distinction. What is the distinction? When God comes to contact man, what man touches is the Spirit. Perhaps some people may ask why it is not enough to say that God is God. Why does the Bible say that God is the Spirit? When God was in the sanctuary, before He came to have a relationship with man, He was purely God. However, when He comes out of His sanctuary to reach and contact man, and when man worships and fellowships with Him, He is the Spirit. In brief, God coming to be touched by man is the Spirit.

THE DISTINCTION BETWEEN SPIRIT AND LIFE

What then is the distinction between the Spirit and life? Life is the content and substance of the Spirit. When the Spirit is received by us, He is life. When we touch the Spirit, we receive life. When God comes out and reaches man, He is the Spirit, and when the Spirit is received and touched by us, He is life. Thus, there are three simple steps that involve three items: God, the Spirit, and life. When God comes out, what we touch is the Spirit. When the Spirit is received and touched by us, He is life. Psalm 36 says that with God is the fountain of life (v. 9). The Gospel of John mentions that this life is in Christ Jesus and that He is the life (1:4; 11:25). Then the Epistles tell us that it is the Spirit who gives life (2 Cor. 3:6), that the Spirit is the Spirit of life (Rom. 8:2), and that when we touch the Spirit, we touch life. They also tell us that to set our mind on the spirit is life (v. 6) and that he who has the Son has the life while he who does not have the Son of God does not have the life (1 John 5:12).

In summary, God is in Christ, and the life of God is in Christ. In Christ is God's life. Christ is also in the Holy Spirit, and this life is in the Holy Spirit. Hence, when the Holy Spirit comes into man, life also comes into man. When man touches the Spirit, he touches life, and when man receives the Spirit, he receives life. In other words, God in the sanctuary is God. But when God comes out to contact us, He is the Spirit, and when the Spirit is received and touched by us, He is life. To say it in reverse, life is the Spirit being received and touched by man.

TOUCHING THE SPIRIT BEING TO TOUCH LIFE

Perhaps some people may ask how we may know when we have contacted the Spirit, when we are living in our spirit, and when we have touched the Spirit. A normal Christian life is a life of living in the Spirit. If we live in the Spirit, we will be living in resurrection. In resurrection are the experiences of death and ascension. Hence, the key to the Christian living is to live in the Spirit. When we live in the Spirit, we will have a condition or feeling of life and peace. Whenever we live in the Spirit, we touch life, because when the Spirit is received by us, He is life. When the Spirit is enjoyed and touched by us, He is life.

Therefore, the greatest proof of our living in the Spirit is that we are receiving, contacting, and touching life. After we receive this life, inwardly there is a kind of condition, taste, and feeling in us that we are fresh, living, strong, and powerful, and we deeply sense the presence of God.

THE FOUR CHARACTERISTICS OF LIFE

Livingness

There are four great characteristics and expressions of the life in us. Once we touch life, there will be four definite expressions, that is, four kinds of conditions or feelings that we will have. First, we will have a sense of livingness. To be living is to be enlivened. Sometimes we are strangely deadened inside. We feel as if we are deflated, and we are unable to be uplifted. This condition is proof that we have not been living in our spirit. When you talk to a brother or pray with a sister, you will know whether this person's spirit is depressed or living. If their spirit is depressed, nothing will come out of them, and they will be unable to pray out their burdens. Whether a person is inwardly deadened or living is especially manifested in prayer. If a person is enlivened when he prays, this proves that he is filled with life inwardly, but if he is unable to utter a word in prayer, this proves that he is disheartened and has not been living in the spirit.

Many saints are unable to open their mouths in the Lord's table meetings and the prayer meetings because they are inwardly deadened and have not been living in the Spirit. Throughout the whole day or the whole week they have been living not in their spirit but in their soul or even in their flesh. They have not been touching their spirit and are not in their spirit, so they are lifeless. When people contact them in the Lord's table meetings and the prayer meetings, they find that they are inwardly deadened and depressed. When they want to pray, they cannot pray, and when they want to speak, they have nothing to speak. However, if throughout the whole week or the whole day they learn to live in their spirit and to touch the spirit, they will surely touch life. Then once they pray, their spirit will come out. Once they pray, they will touch life because their spirit will be living.

It is the same with those who speak for God on the podium. If they have not turned to their spirit or touched their spirit, they will dry up after a few sentences because they are cut off from the source of life in them. When we are in the spirit, we touch life, and the first expression of life is livingness. Our determination to pray more will not enliven our spirit. The only way for us to be enlivened is to turn from our outer man back to our inner man. Once we touch the Spirit inwardly, we touch life.

The Spirit is life, and life is the Spirit. The Spirit is God coming out to be touched by us, and life is the Spirit coming into us to be received and touched by us. Our spirit is our inner man, whereas our soul and our flesh are the outer man. If a Christian lives in his outer man all the time, living by his flesh, his soul, and his mind, emotion, and will, and does not turn to his inner man, he will be in death and will not touch life. Whenever man touches the Spirit, he lives, because it is the Spirit who gives life (John 6:63). In this verse the Greek word for *life* is used as a verb, indicating that the Holy Spirit "lifes" man. The Holy Spirit is life itself. Once He contacts us and touches us inwardly, He "lifes" us. It is the Spirit who gives life because the Holy Spirit Himself is life.

The Spirit is not in our thoughts, in our emotion, in our mind, or in our flesh. Rather, He is in our spirit. Whenever we are in our outer man, we are unable to contact the Spirit or touch life, but whenever we turn back to our spirit, we contact the Spirit and touch life. This is like an electrical switch. If we take off the cover from an electrical switch and touch the electrical wire, once we touch the electrical wire, we touch the electricity itself because the electricity is in the electrical wire. In the same way, the Spirit of life is in our spirit. Every time we turn to our spirit to touch the Spirit, we touch life, and once we touch life, we are "lifed," that is, we live and become strong. Immediately, we will rise up from our feeling of depression, and our deadness will be made living. Hence, the first expression of life is livingness.

Freshness

The second expression of life is freshness. What is it to be fresh? To be fresh is to be vigorous and living. When you meet a saint with the appearance of oldness, you know that he has not been living in the Spirit. One who lives in the Spirit is renewed daily and never gets old. A certain saint once testified that in 1933 he met an elderly Christian brother in Europe. This elderly brother was already over eighty years of age at that time and was not able to hear well. But when the saint fellowshipped with this brother, he enjoyed his spiritual freshness. According to his physical body, this elderly brother was not able to hear or speak much, but when people came to him, they could sense his inward freshness. This elderly man would hold the saint's hand steadily and firmly and say, "Brother, to this day I cannot live without Him, and He cannot live without me." Who is this "He"? This "He" is the Lord. How sweet a statement this is: "I cannot live without Him, and He cannot live without me." These two sentences are so fresh! This brother did not need to use thousands of words. Rather, in two sentences he was able to cause others to touch God. This proves that he was inwardly living and fresh and had the presence of God.

Brightness

The third expression of life is brightness. One who lives in the Spirit and touches the Spirit will be bright. There was once a famous preacher. By reading his writings, you could not get a sense of his person; however, when you listened to his speaking for the Lord on the podium, you could realize that he was as transparent as glass and as clear as crystal. This was because he was a man in the spirit.

Sometimes when you contact a person, you feel like you are touching a wall, a big stone, or a cave. Once you contact him, you have an unfortunate feeling. You feel as if you have fallen into a cave, an underground vault, or some place that is very dark and without any light or brightness. At other times, however, when you meet someone else and spend a brief amount of time with him, you feel that there is light and that everything is bright. The reason that a person lacks brightness is not because he does not have life within but because he is not living in the Spirit. Once a person lives in the Spirit, he touches the Spirit and has life because the Spirit is life. Life is the light that shines on man (cf. John 1:4). Once we touch life, this life is light. This is the third expression of life.

Strength

The fourth expression of life is strength. Life is powerful and does not fear anything. The wind cannot hurt life. Rather, it helps life to grow. The reason grass does not grow well sometimes is that it is not exposed to sunlight or wind. The places where grass grows well are the places where there is ample sunlight and moderate wind. Many times the exposure to sunlight, the blowing of the wind, and the beating of the rain do not destroy life. Instead, they help life to grow because life is strong and powerful.

There was once a certain person who was stumbled because the usher arranged for him to sit under a fan in the meeting. Because of this he never came to the meeting again. This is a weak Christian. We must realize that when a man is weak to the uttermost, he dies. Death is the expression of someone who is weak to the uttermost. The more living a person is, the stronger he is and the more life-energy he has, because life causes man to be strong. If we are such people, we will not be stumbled if we are asked to sit under a fan. We will not fall even if we are put in the basement. With life, the more the difficulties, the stronger the wind, and the harder the rain, the more it will grow. May the Lord have mercy on us to strengthen us that our expression may prove that we are living in spirit and in life.

LIFE AND PEACE

Finally, these four points added together issue in peace and satisfaction, not emptiness or poverty. The living of some Christians is empty, dissatisfied, uneasy, uncomfortable, and rough, as if a hand were grasping them every day. Sometimes when they want to go to a movie, it is as if a hand grabs them from within. When they want to quarrel with others, a hand again grabs them from within. After they have quarreled with someone, they may lie on their bed, and even though the bed is restful, their inner being is unrestful because a hand is still grasping them. When they come to the meeting, they feel uneasy whether they sit or stand. When the bread is broken, everyone is joyful, but they can neither cry nor smile. It is as if they are suspended in mid-air. This kind of Christian does not have rest, peace, or joy because he has not touched the spirit or received life. Romans 8:6 says that when we touch the spirit, we touch life; and when life comes, peace is there.

The issue of these four conditions or expressions is peace. Peace includes satisfaction. Once we touch life, our inner being becomes living, fresh, bright, strong, and satisfied. Once we are satisfied, we have peace within. Whether we sit or stand, we have peace. Even when we are sitting in an uncomfortable place, we have peace. When we come to the Lord's table meeting, we are all the more joyful. We are able to praise the Lord and say amen to others' praises. The reason we can have such peace is that we are satisfied, and the reason we are satisfied is that we are living, fresh, bright, and strong within. This is the sphere and the realm of our Christian living and the beautiful condition of our being in spirit and in life.

CHAPTER NINE

THE SPIRIT BEING OUR LIFE

HAVING SPIRITUAL REALITY
ONLY BY TOUCHING THE SPIRIT OF GOD

The Holy Spirit Himself is our spiritual life. When we touch the Holy Spirit inwardly and experience the Holy Spirit, He becomes our spiritual life and our spiritual living. The spiritual life is spiritual reality. All spiritual reality is the issue of the Spirit of God touching our spirit. The resulting expression is love, humility, work, power, wisdom, brightness, revelation, and vision. Hence, the entire Christian living and work is an expression of spiritual reality.

Spiritual reality is the Spirit of God touching our spirit and being our life in our spirit. Such a life produces various kinds of expressions. These expressions are our spiritual living and even our spiritual work.

THE EXPRESSION OF THE SPIRITUAL LIFE

Imitation Not Being
the Expression of the Spiritual Life

What is the expression of the spiritual life? Suppose there is a brother who is humble and meek. Suppose another brother admires the way he lives such a life of humility and meekness and resolves to make himself live in the same way, being humble and meek in all things. He even prays to the Lord that he would live a life of humility and meekness. He has morning watch, reads the Bible, prays, acts carefully and cautiously, and does not get puffed up or irritated. Thus, by receiving the supply and help from that humble and meek brother, he also becomes humble and meek. In other words, because he is close to the humble and meek brother, he also becomes a humble and meek person.

This, however, is not spiritual reality or a genuine spiritual living. This is merely an imitation. Although humanly speaking this kind of behavior seems precious, normal, and proper, in terms of spiritual reality, it is not spiritual, and it is not the expression of the living out of the Lord's life. Instead, it comes entirely from man's own effort of self-cultivation. Only when the Spirit of God touches our spirit is something genuine produced—spiritual reality, the expression of life, and a genuine spiritual living.

Suppose there is a saint who decides that he will open his mouth to pray in the prayer meeting. Thus, before the meeting he remembers to prepare himself well and to ask the Lord for strength. Then when he comes to the meeting, in his heart he is thinking all the time that he has to pray. After the first hymn, due to his nervousness and considerations, all the opportunities for prayer are taken away. Then after the second hymn, because too many people are touched to pray, when he stands up and is about to open his mouth, other people are already giving thanks and praising. So he sits down again and waits for another opportunity. Then before the end of the last hymn, he suddenly stands up to pray using nice phrases in a loud and clear voice. When the people hear this, they echo with loud amens. However, such a prayer is not the expression of life or the living of spiritual reality. Rather, it is the result of human effort.

Zeal Not Being the Expression of the Spiritual Life

There are some people who are always thinking of other brothers and sisters and who want to have more fellowship with them. They fellowship with someone one day and talk with another one the next day. They never stop fellowshipping and talking with people day after day. For others, visiting people is a burden, but for them, visiting people is not a burden at all. For others, it is inconvenient to go to visit people, but for them it is miserable to be unable to go to visit people. Others are reluctant to visit people, but they spontaneously visit people. They sympathize with those who are weak, those who have stumbled, and those who have difficulties. Thus, they fellowship with one person one day and comfort another one the next day. They talk to one person in the morning and speak to another one in the afternoon. They are always diligently visiting and fellowshipping with the brothers and sisters. The responsible brothers may even praise them for their zeal. However, this is neither spiritual reality nor the expression of genuine spiritual living. Rather, it is the zeal of the flesh. This kind of zeal and diligence is of the flesh. It is not produced from being touched by the Spirit of God, nor is it the expression of the spiritual life.

Perhaps some people may turn around and say that if humility and meekness are not spiritual reality but only cultivated behavior, then we should not be humble or meek. Although this kind of living would eliminate cultivated behavior, it would result in an unruly kind of living, which would be even worse. Perhaps some people may think that if deciding to open our mouths and pray in the meeting is only human effort, then we should not pray in the meeting. Instead, we should neglect our responsibility and just sit there comfortably, fully at ease without opening our mouth. While this would eliminate human effort, it would bring in human looseness. In response to this fellowship, we should not say that we are merely criticizing everything we do, saying that we are wrong whether we move or do not move. On the one hand, if we fellowship with people and visit them wherever they are, others will say that this is the zeal of the flesh. On the other hand, if we stop all our activities and do none of these things, others will say that we are loose. How then should we live and work?

THE SPIRITUAL LIFE BEING EXPRESSED ONLY WHEN THE HUMAN SPIRIT TOUCHES THE SPIRIT OF GOD

Genuine spiritual living is the issue or expression that is produced by our spirit touching the Spirit of God. When our spirit touches the Spirit, the issue or expression is our humility, our meekness, our prayer, our love toward the saints, and our visiting the saints. When all these human virtues are expressed in our daily living as the issue of the Spirit of God touching our spirit, they are spiritual reality and the genuine spiritual living.

Hence, spiritual reality is the issue that is produced from the Spirit of God touching our spirit. God as the Spirit comes to contact us, and when the Spirit enters into us to be touched and experienced by us, He becomes our spiritual life.

GOD, CHRIST, THE HOLY SPIRIT, AND LIFE BEING INSEPARABLE

John 10:10 tells us that the Lord came that we may have life. Chapter one verse 4 says that in Him was life, and Colossians 3:4 says, "Christ our life." We are all familiar with these verses, and we often say that the Lord is our life and that once we touch the Lord, we touch life. However, the saints may still find this matter vague. How is it that when we touch the Lord, we touch life? How can the Lord be our life? How can we practically experience the Lord's life? All the saints have these questions. According to the revelation in the Scriptures, we see that God causes us to receive His life through Christ, in whom is life. One day this life flowed out from Christ. In the Old Testament a rock was smitten and cleft, and out from the rock came the living water (Exo. 17:6). The rock signifies Christ, while the living water signifies the Holy Spirit (1 Cor. 10:4; cf. John 7:37-38). The rock being cleft and living water coming out signify that Christ was crucified and that the water that came out of Him was the Holy Spirit. When the Holy Spirit comes into us, He is life, and this life is the Holy Spirit. Just as God and the Spirit are one, the Spirit and life are also one (Rom. 8:2). We must see that the Holy Spirit who comes out of the Lord is the life that enters into us. The Holy Spirit is life.

God, Christ, the Holy Spirit, and life are not separate entities. God is Christ, Christ is the Holy Spirit, and the Holy Spirit is life. This means that God is in Christ, Christ is in the Holy Spirit, and the Holy Spirit is in life. When we touch life, we touch the Holy Spirit. When we touch the Holy Spirit, we touch Christ. When we touch Christ, we touch God. Regarding the Holy Spirit, the Holy Spirit is the Spirit of life that causes man to have life. Life is in the Holy Spirit, and when we touch the Holy Spirit, we touch life. Regarding life, life is God, life is Christ, and life is the Holy Spirit. Specifically, life is the Spirit, the Spirit is Christ, and Christ is God. Therefore, life is God. One thing we need to mention, however, is that it is in Christ that God becomes our life and that it is in the Holy Spirit that Christ is received by us. When we receive Christ in the Holy Spirit, we receive life, and when we touch Christ in the Holy Spirit, we touch life.

God, Christ, the Holy Spirit, and life are not four separate entities but one. When we have one, we have the other three. God, Christ, and the Holy Spirit are experienced and received by us in life. Specifically, life is in the Holy Spirit, and the Holy Spirit enables us to receive life, touch life, and experience life. Hence, when we touch the Holy Spirit, we experience life and touch life. Therefore, we must realize that we cannot touch the Spirit by thinking in our mind, feeling with our emotion, or deciding in our will. Only when we turn to our innermost part can we touch the Spirit. This innermost part is deeper than our mind, emotion, and will. This innermost part is our spirit. Only when we are in the spirit can we touch the Spirit of God.

BEING A CHRISTIAN FROM WITHIN

We should be Christians inwardly, not merely outwardly. The outward things refer to our mind, emotion, and will and to all the outward activities. This is similar to the two levels of Chinese boxing. On one level you develop the outward skills, learning the correct postures and stances, but after learning these things, you still may not hit the mark. On the other level you develop the internal strength that enables you to hit the crucial point of your opponent with a fist. It is the same with Christians. Some people preach unceasingly and at great length, but you may feel that the words they speak float in the air and do not touch your deepest feeling. Some people, however, may not speak much, and their words may be simple, but their words can enter into your deepest part. When you go home, their words and their messages still prick you in your heart. Why is that? It is because those words came from their inner being, their spirit, which is deeper than their mind, emotion, and will.

As Christians, we should first develop our "internal strength" and then our "outward skills." For example, when a person kneels down to pray in the morning, he may have a set prayer. Either he does not pray, or once he prays, he recites a whole set of prayers. In the past the Chinese had to read books such as *The Three-Character Classic,* the *Book of Family Names, The Analects,* and the *Book of Mencius* and had to memorize them one by one. The prayers of some Christians are similar to the reciting of *The Three-Character Classic* or the *Book of Family Names.* Although this may not be wrong, the question is whether the Lord is "wearing" them and praying in them in their prayers, or whether they are praying according to their own will. The elders have their own set of prayers, the ones who are responsible for the home meetings have their own set of prayers, the deacons have their set of prayers, the brothers have their set of prayers, and the sisters have their set of prayers. Once they open their mouths, we know almost exactly what they are going to say. This kind of prayer may be only a religious prayer, a religious ritual, and a religious formality.

Our prayer should come from our turning to our spirit and touching our spirit. Many of our prayers are formal—not in spirit but apart from our spirit. Formal prayers are surely of the mind, emotion, and will. Hence, we must rid ourselves of these formalities and turn from the outside to the inside. When we pray from the deepest part of our being, we spontaneously touch the intention of God and cooperate with Him outwardly in action.

TURNING FROM OUR MIND, EMOTION, AND WILL INTO OUR SPIRIT

When we come to the Lord, we should not stay in our mind. Rather, we should pray directly to the Lord according to our inner sense. For example, in the Lord's table meeting, the prayers of the brothers and sisters are precious, but they often just repeat one another. One time a brother stood up and prayed, "O Lord, we thank and praise You. We are here around Your table and see how great Your love is!" After he finished his set of prayers, a sister stood up and prayed, "O Lord, we really thank and praise You. We break the bread to remember You." These words were not from the spirit but from the mind. They were set prayers. Some brothers and sisters are more capable. They are able to memorize many doctrines concerning the Lord's being born as a man, His living on the earth for thirty-three and a half years, His crucifixion, His death, His resurrection, His ascension, His becoming a High Priest and a Mediator, His interceding for us in the heavens, and His second coming. The more they pray, however, the lower the spirits of the saints sink. Eventually, no one is able to even say amen. For this reason, we need to have our mind, emotion, and will broken so that we may enter into our innermost part to pray.

As saved ones, we have been enlivened in our spirit. The Spirit of the Lord, Christ, the almighty God, and the resurrection life are all in our spirit. When we turn from our mind, emotion, and will to our spirit, we touch God. Although sometimes it is not that easy to touch Him at the beginning, we do not need to be anxious. When a car is first started, the engine is cold, but after a short while, the engine begins to warm up. Hence, the more we pray, the more our spirit will be stirred up, and the more we pray, the more our spirit will be burning. Throughout the day, we have to exercise to turn from our mind, emotion, and will to our spirit and learn to stay in and be calm in our spirit to touch the Spirit. Once we touch the Spirit, we touch life, and we receive life. This is spiritual reality. Only what comes from within, from the spirit, is genuine spiritual reality.

CHAPTER TEN

HOW TO LIVE A PRACTICAL SPIRITUAL LIFE

A PRACTICAL SPIRITUAL LIFE

Ephesians 3:17 says that Christ makes His home in our hearts through faith in order that, as verse 19 says, we may be filled unto all the fullness of God. The issue of Christ's making His home in our hearts is that we are filled unto all the fullness of God. The unique goal that God desires to accomplish in us who are saved is to work Himself into us and to work us into Him so that He and we, we and He, would be mingled as one.

Spiritual reality is the result of the Spirit of God touching the spirit of man. This means that the proper and genuine Christian living is the living that issues from our spirit touching the Spirit of God. The way we conduct ourselves in our life, our living, our work, and all of our actions should be the issue of our spirit touching the Spirit of God and not the issue of our relying on ourselves. If we live by ourselves and rely on ourselves, then strictly speaking, our living is not the living of a Christian but the living of an ordinary person or, at the most, the living of a religious person. People in general regard Christians, or those who believe in Jesus, as religious people. Actually, those who truly know the Lord's salvation and live in spiritual reality by the grace of God have their living mingled together with God.

God is true and living, and the Spirit is also true and living. Just as God is real, the Spirit is also real and spiritual, not empty or vague. The Spirit of God has come into our spirit, and once our spirit touches the Spirit of God, there is an effect. This effect enables us as saved Christians to have a certain kind of living—the Christian living. This kind of living is in spirit and in resurrection, and this kind of living is spiritual reality.

THREE KINDS OF LIVING

Generally speaking, there are three kinds of living. First, there is an ethical living; second, there is a religious living; and third, there is a spiritual living. A person should at the very least have an ethical living. As those who live in human society, we should be ethical people. This should be obvious. Second, an upright person should have a religious belief and a religious living. It is generally acknowledged that those who have a religious living are nobler than those who merely have an ethical living. However, the purpose of God's salvation is not to make us merely ethical or religious people. The purpose of God's salvation is something higher than this. It is not enough to be either ethical or religious. God's purpose in His salvation is to work in us to the extent that we would have a kind of living that surpasses the ethical and religious living. This kind of living is a spiritual living.

A spiritual living is a result of our spirit touching the Spirit of God. Often a spiritual living may appear similar to an ethical and religious living, but actually an ethical and religious living is not a spiritual living. For example, outwardly brass looks like gold, but it is not gold. The expression of a spiritual living is similar to that of an ethical and religious living. However, an ethical and religious living is not a spiritual living but a living of the human will. There is no spiritual element or flavor in an ethical and religious living because there is no spiritual reality or weight in it.

An Ethical Living

What is an ethical and religious living, and how is it different from a spiritual living? For most of us, what we live out every day is either ethical or religious. For example, a husband's relationship to his wife may be mostly ethical, and a wife's relationship to her husband may be mostly ethical. A husband may have the concept that as an upright man, and particularly as one who believes in the Lord Jesus, he should love his wife, sympathize with her, be considerate toward her, and take care of her. According to his concept this is the way to fulfill the requirements of being a husband. The wife may have the concept that she should be submissive to her husband, respect her husband, and not quarrel with him, or else she will not meet the biblical standard of a wife. The children may have the concept that they should honor their parents, obey them, and respect them, and that they should not be careless in their attitude and speaking toward them. This is filial piety, which is one of the most important items in an ethical living. Most of us are just like this. We do not act loosely but are ethical toward our relatives, colleagues, classmates, and the saints in the church. We have the thought that since we are upright people who believe in the Lord, our living should be proper, regulated, careful, and serious.

An ethical living is merely the good that a man does. It is not the result of man's touching God, nor does it require man to touch God. An atheist can be an upright person and behave uprightly yet be entirely apart from God. This kind of upright behavior is an ethical living. It is a living that is apart from God and that has no need of God. This kind of upright living is the highest kind of living among the unbelievers. The unbelievers focus on ethics, but they do not have God, nor do they worship or serve God.

Then how do we describe our living? We believe in God, pray to God, worship God, and serve God. Many times we also rely on God. We may have the desire to be ethical, but we do not have the ability to be ethical. We may desire to do good, but we are not able to do it. Hence, we are always praying that God would grant us strength in times of temptation and that He would help and support us so that we would be able to stand. From this we see that in our living there is more or less some flavor of God, something that issues from the help of God.

The purpose of God's salvation in us is to save us to such an extent that we would not only be moral but that the nature of our morality would be the mingling of God with us. In other words, we would no longer be "brass" but "gold." We would have not only the outward appearance but also the

inward substance, and the nature of our morality would not
be out of man but of God. It would be the mingling of God and
man. Real morality in God's salvation is produced by our
spirit touching the Spirit of God.

A Spiritual Living

Our living may be upright and ethical, but is our walk and
upright condition produced by our spirit touching the Spirit
of God, or is it unnecessary for us to touch the Spirit of God
in order to have such a living? This makes a big difference. In
our daily life, a spiritual living can be produced only by our
spirit touching the Spirit of God. Only when the spirit of man
touches the Spirit of God will there be spiritual reality. We
should check our experience. How many of the proper, upright,
and even ethical things that we do throughout the day are
produced by our spirit touching the Spirit of God? We need to
ask God to be gracious to us and to enlighten us so that we
may see that today as Christians it is a matter of the Spirit of
God living in our spirit. We need to interact and mingle with
the Spirit of God in our spirit that we may live in the spirit
day by day.

In this way, as soon as we get up in the morning, we will
spontaneously be in the spirit. We will come to God and interact with the Spirit of God by the spirit. Then throughout the
entire day we must remain in the spirit and walk according to
the spirit. We should honor our parents the way our spirit
wants us to honor our parents. We should treat our husband
the way our spirit wants us to treat our husband. We should
love our wife the way our spirit wants us to love our wife. In
whatever way our spirit wants us to love, to be sympathetic,
and to be meek and humble toward people, we should take
that way, and spontaneously we will live according to the feeling of our spirit. Then what will come forth will not be merely
an ethical living or a spiritual living but a spiritual living
that includes an ethical living. This kind of morality is much
higher than morality by itself. Sadly, many Christians do not
have much of the spiritual element in their living. Their
honor toward their parents comes from them, not from touching the spirit. Their sympathy and love toward others are

merely their own sympathy and love and do not come from touching the Spirit of God. Their kind of living does not have God or any spiritual element in it.

A Religious Living

In addition to an ethical living and a spiritual living, there is a religious living. If we have a religious living, we will get up in the morning and pray regardless of whether or not we touch the spirit, as if prayer were a regulation, an obligation, or a religious ritual. We pray, but we do not touch the spirit. Instead, we merely recite a prayer from our mind. This kind of prayer is religious prayer, and this kind of living is a religious living. It is the same with praying before meals. We may be bothered if we do not pray, but when we do pray, we do not touch the spirit. We merely put our heads down, close our eyes, and say a few sentences of thanks and praise. This is a religious ritual. This is the prayer of religious people. They feel uneasy when they do not pray, but nothing happens after they pray. Many times our prayers are the same. Our prayers are religious and ritualistic and do not touch the spirit. Of course, if some people touch the spirit when they pray before meals, then their prayer is not ritualistic. But for the majority of Christians, praying before meals is merely part of a religious living, because in their prayers they do not touch God. Anything that we do without being touched in our spirit is part of a religious living.

We may be doing activities that are seemingly spiritual, such as distributing gospel tracts, preaching the gospel, and visiting people, but if we are doing them without touching the spirit, then they do not have any spiritual weight or spiritual element. If we are not moved in the spirit, then our outward gospel preaching is a religious ritual; it is an aspect of the religious living. If our spirit does not touch the Spirit, then even our coming to the meetings may be an aspect of a religious living. While the unbelievers watch television or play mah-jongg after work, we Christians rush to the meeting hall to attend meetings. However, if our spirit is not moved and does not touch God, we are just the same as the unbelievers.

This kind of meeting life may actually be part of our religious living.

Any aspect of our living that is not a result of our spirit touching the Spirit of God is part of either an ethical living or a religious living. We can live out these two kinds of living without fellowshipping with God, without the Spirit of God, and without the exercise of our spirit. Our daily living and work must come from our spirit touching the Spirit of God and must come from our spirit. Our humility should be the result of our spirit touching the Spirit of God. Our love should come from our spirit touching the Spirit of God. When our spirit touches the Spirit of God and when we fellowship with the Spirit of God, the Spirit of God will move us and urge us so that we cannot help but love man. This kind of love does not come merely from us but is produced from our fellowship with God, our union with God, and our contact with the Spirit of God.

LIVING IN THE SPIRIT, FOLLOWING THE SPIRIT, AND OBEYING THE SPIRIT

A normal, genuine, and spiritual Christian living is the issue of the spirit of man touching the Spirit of God. Before we were saved and had God dwelling in us, it seemed sufficient for us merely to do good. We were used to living in the way of doing good. After we are saved and begin to live a spiritual living, we may encounter some problems and may be unaccustomed to a spiritual living. Gradually, however, we will begin to learn not to live by ourselves but to turn to our spirit and to think of God in our living. Eventually we will reach a point where we may not even deliberately exercise our spirit to touch the Spirit of God; because our heart is proper and because we are always in fellowship with God and because of His moving within us, we will spontaneously touch the Spirit of God. The Bible tells us that this moving is the anointing in us. The anointing touches our spirit, joins to our spirit, and motivates us. When we live a life according to this motivation, we will be living a spiritual living. All of our actions and behavior, being the result of our following and obeying the Holy Spirit, will not merely be ethical or religious but spiritual. This kind of living is the Christian living—a living that is spiritual, genuine, and proper. It is also a living that is spiritual reality.

THE OBSTACLES TO LIVING
A PRACTICAL SPIRITUAL LIFE

Being Unwilling to Stop Our Self
and to Deny Our Soul

There are two obstacles to living a practical spiritual life. The first obstacle is the unwillingness to stop our self and to deny our soul. Instead of stopping our self, we often may continue to act according to our own will. We may continue to think what we want to think, love what we want to love, and choose what we want to choose. We may completely ignore our spirit. We may have heard the spiritual doctrines many times, but we may remain unchanged, still living by ourselves and being unwilling to stop ourselves. This is a big problem.

We need to be enlightened and saved to see that the most detestable matter concerning us is not the fact that we still sin or love the world. It is the fact that we cannot stop our self. Most of us are still living in ourselves. Our mind, emotion, and will are still ruling us, and we are still living by our soul. Although we have been saved and enlivened and have the Spirit of God in us, we still put the spirit aside and live by our mind, emotion, preferences, and ideas. Thus, our first obstacle is that it is hard for us to stop ourselves and deny our soul.

A Conditional Submission

The second obstacle is that our submission to the feeling of the spirit may be conditional. When we live by the spirit, the Spirit of God is living, strong, and powerful, but we still may not fully submit to Him. The Spirit of God operates in us by inwardly moving in us, forbidding us, directing us, controlling us, dealing with us, and requiring things of us. He may require us to get rid of some things and to deal with other things. He may require us to deny our self, to come out of our flesh, to turn to our spirit, and to submit to the feeling in our spirit. This is the Spirit's moving, operating, forbidding, directing, controlling, dealing, and requiring in our spirit. When we experience this, we may discover that when the moving and operating match our taste, we submit, but when they do not match our taste, we find it difficult and burdensome to submit. The question that we must ask ourselves is, "Are we willing to submit?" Our unwillingness to submit is the problem. The genuine submission of a Christian is to submit to the spirit and to touch the feeling of the spirit.

For example, there once was a Christian who had a friend that he was very close to. If he had to go for a long time without seeing his friend, it was upsetting to him. This Christian was endeavoring to live in his spirit to contact and fellowship with the Spirit, so at a certain point the Holy Spirit began to move and operate in his spirit. Whenever the Holy Spirit asked him to pray, to praise, to meet, or to do good, he was very happy, but whenever the Holy Spirit moved, operated, and touched him regarding his friend, he found it hard to submit. Whenever he was about to go visit his friend, the Holy Spirit forbade him. Whenever he was about to invite his friend to visit him, his inner being did not allow him. He had the clear feeling that although he had been able to visit his friend as he pleased in the past, now the Holy Spirit within him would not allow him to go to see his friend in the same way. Hence, he was in a dilemma concerning whether to submit or not. The feeling in his spirit was requiring him to put his friend aside, but emotionally he was absolutely unwilling to put him aside. Thus, he disobeyed the inner feeling, discarded the moving of the Holy Spirit, allowed his emotions to rule him, and followed his emotions to go to see his friend. In short, he turned from his spirit to his soul, and immediately he lost his fellowship with God. Outwardly he had not committed a great sin or an evil act, and even his family had agreed that he should be friends with this upright person, but because he chose to live in his soul and not in his spirit, he lost the presence of the Spirit and the fellowship of the Spirit.

Spiritual matters are like an electric lamp. When we turn the switch on, the lamp shines. It may seem quite complicated to talk about the Spirit of God, about incarnation bringing God into man, about death and resurrection bringing man into God, and about the experience of death and ascension in resurrection. However, these matters are very simple to experience. Normally, we speak, walk, and live in our soul. We love, give opinions, and make decisions entirely in the soul. Whatever our soul decides, we do, and whatever our soul thinks, we think. But now that we see that deep within us we have a spirit and that the Spirit of God is in our spirit, when we fellowship and contact God in our spirit, the Spirit of God will touch our spirit, and eventually we will obey and follow the feeling in our spirit. This is the Christian living. When this happens, the living that we live out will not be merely an ethical or religious living but a spiritual living. When we have this living, we will live in the spirit, have spiritual reality, and live a life of mingling with God. Then God's eternal purpose will be accomplished in us.

Spiritual Reality Depending on Turning from Our Soul to Our Spirit

Our problem is that it is not easy for us to turn from the outward to the inward, that is, from our soul to our spirit. For example, we may be used to lighting kerosene lamps for light. Thus, even though we have electric lights installed in our homes, we still light the kerosene lamps. Spiritual reality depends not on how many messages we listen to, how much we pray, or how much we meet. Rather, it depends on whether or not we are willing to put our soul aside and exercise our spirit. The key is whether or not we are willing to have our being transferred from our soul to our spirit, and whether or not we are willing to turn our being around, turning it from our soul back to our spirit. Our need is to turn from our soul to our spirit. When we turn from our soul to our spirit, we will touch the Spirit of God in our spirit and will have some feeling within. Once we have this feeling, we should submit to it. In whatever way the Spirit moves in us, we should obey. If we do so, we will be the most blessed people.

When we submit in this way, all the riches of God will fill us inwardly day after day. God's power, God's life, God's virtues, God's love, God's light, and all the riches in God will be wrought into our being little by little, filling us within. The main reason we do not always have light within and are often confused, unclear, and darkened is that we do not turn to our spirit. If we are willing to turn to our spirit, our inner being will be enlightened, and our understanding will be opened. We will be able to see revelations every day and know what pleases or displeases the Lord. Then we will deal with the matters that need to be dealt with and follow the feelings that we receive. In this way the life in us will grow, and our Bible reading will be full of light and full of taste.

In the past we may have only known to recite the letter of the Bible with our mind, but we may not have seen the light and revelation in the Bible. However, the more we grow in life, are opened in our understanding, and have the presence of the Holy Spirit with the reality of resurrection, the more we will have the light and revelation in our spirit. Furthermore, we will be able to touch God's feeling regarding our future, our job, our conduct, and our management of the affairs of the church. Many people say that it is difficult to know God's will. The more they pray, the more confused they are. This is because they are accustomed to living by their soul in their daily living. They do not pray unless something happens to them. The reason why they become more confused the more they pray is because they are so accustomed to living in their soul. Thus, when things happen to them, they are unable to pray in the spirit. If we always exercise in our daily life to deny our soul and live in our spirit to fellowship with God, then when something happens to us, it will be easy for us to touch God's desire within.

SPIRITUAL REVELATION, SHINING, SIGHT, AND VISION

These four matters—spiritual revelation, spiritual shining, spiritual sight, and spiritual vision—are apparently similar but are actually very different. For example, suppose that there is a certain object hidden in a bag and that we can see the bag but cannot see what is inside the bag. Revelation is the opening of the bag, showing what is within. The Greek word for *revelation* means "to open the veil." For instance, in a theater there is a veil that covers the scenery on the stage. When the show begins, the veil is lifted up so that we may see the scenery. This is revelation, an unveiling.

However, we may not be able to see even when there is revelation. If there is no light in the theater and everything is dark, although the veil may be lifted, we still will not see the scenery. Moreover, if a person is blind and his eyes cannot be opened, then there may be revelation and shining, but due to his blindness he will not have the vision either. He may have revelation and shining, but he may not have vision, because he has no sight. When there is revelation, shining, and opened eyes, then there will be vision. A vision is an extraordinary scene. Revelation is the unveiling of a certain thing, shining is what enables the eyes to see, and the result of seeing is a vision.

Many people talk about the Bible, but they do not know that there is revelation in the Bible. As a result, they spend much time talking about the Bible without seeing any revelation or vision. These people are mostly in their soul, not in their spirit. They have no experience of life or inward light and are neither enlightened nor opened in their understanding. Even though they read the Bible again and again, they still cannot see the revelation. Revelation is there, but due to the lack of light and vision, they cannot see. Only a certain kind of people—those who turn from their soul to their spirit and who continually learn to walk according to God in their spirit—will have the light and the sight. These people have the riches of God in their spirit, and when they live in their spirit, they have light and life. Every time they come to read the Bible, the Bible is bright and shining to them. In their daily living, they find it easy to touch the feeling of the spirit. In this way, day by day they are those who live in the spirit, who live in God, and who are filled unto all the fullness of God. This is the goal that God wants to accomplish in us. May we all press on toward this goal.

Chapter Eleven

THE VISION AND THE WAY
OF THE UNION OF GOD AND MAN

Scripture Reading: Matt. 1:23; John 14:20-23; 17:21-23; 1 John 3:24; 1 Cor. 6:17; Rom. 8:9-10; Eph. 3:17a, 19b; Col. 2:9-10a; Rev. 21:1-3

SERVING THE LORD
ACCORDING TO SPIRITUAL VISION

Everyone who pursues and serves the Lord should have a basic spiritual vision, a basic spiritual seeing. A person who pursues the Lord should not serve the Lord according to his natural feeling, his natural insight, or his natural view.

All those who serve God according to their natural insight cannot truly serve or touch God. Saul of Tarsus was one who served God fervently, but he served God in a natural way, not according to revelation. Thus, his service could not truly serve or touch God. One day on his way to Damascus his eyes were opened to see a vision. Then he began to bring forth genuine service, service that reached God. Formerly he had served God, but his service could not touch God. This may be likened to boxing. In the past he had been beating the air, but then his eyes were opened to see how he should box. It is the same with the matter of pursuing the Lord. Some people pursue but fail to obtain what they are pursuing. Some may even shed tears in their desperation, but they still fail to obtain what they are pursuing. The reason is that they are pursuing according to their naturalness, their own feeling, and their own insight. They are pursuing for their own interests and by their own inclination, without any revelation, seeing, or vision. They are running in vain and laboring fruitlessly because their eyes have not been opened.

Hence, we cannot say that pursuing the Lord is good enough. The pursuits of many people are empty pursuits, their prayers are empty prayers, and even their shedding of tears is in vain, because they pray according to their own inclination, pursue according to their own insight, and shed tears according to their own feeling. Everything they do is natural, without any revelation. Thus, their pursuit is a waste of effort because they have not pursued what they should pursue and have not obtained what they should obtain. Therefore, in spiritual matters, we must have sight, vision, and revelation.

THE VISION OF THE MINGLING OF GOD AND MAN

The first spiritual vision we need to see is the vision of the mingling of God and man. God has a desire to mingle Himself with man. Although we cannot find such a statement in either the Old or the New Testament, this fact is clearly revealed from Genesis all the way to Revelation.

THE FIRST AND THE LAST TIMES
MAN IS MENTIONED IN THE BIBLE

The first mention of man in the Bible is in Genesis 1, which speaks of how man was created in the image of God. Why did God create man in His image? God created man in His image because God's purpose is to mingle Himself with man. Thus, when He created man, He created man just like Him. We can play with a dog, but that dog cannot be our intimate friend because it is different from us. We simply cannot become close friends with a dog. In the beginning God created man in His image and made man just like Him because His intention is that man would be a vessel to contain Him.

The last mention of man in the Bible is in Revelation 21, which describes the New Jerusalem in the new heaven and new earth. In this chapter three different titles are used to depict man. First, man is called the New Jerusalem; second, he is called the wife of the Lamb; and third, man is the tabernacle of God in which God dwells (vv. 2-3, 9).

GOD BEING WITH MAN

Revelation is the last book of the Bible. Many of the important types that are mentioned in Genesis to Jude are fulfilled in Revelation. When God called the children of Israel and formed them into a nation, He raised up something special among them—the building of the Tent of Meeting. The Tent of Meeting in the Old Testament refers to the tabernacle. This tabernacle was erected in the midst of the children of Israel, and God dwelt in it. After the children of Israel entered Canaan, the tabernacle became the temple. The tabernacle in the wilderness was mobile, but when it became the temple in the land of Canaan, it became stationary. The tabernacle and the temple are of the same nature. The tabernacle was a type, typifying the dwelling place of God among men and His mingling with man. In Revelation 21 the New Jerusalem, typified by the tabernacle, is practically accomplished. Although the New Jerusalem is a city, it is the dwelling place of God among men throughout the ages and is typified by the tabernacle. Hence, the New Jerusalem is the totality of God's dwelling place among men.

In the New Jerusalem the Lamb is the temple of God because God is in Christ the Lamb (v. 22). Christ with God dwells in the New Jerusalem, which is the eternal dwelling place of God among men. Hence, on the one hand the New Jerusalem is a city, and on the other hand it is a group of people. The city as the dwelling place of God is a group of people—the bride of the Lamb and the wife of the Lamb. The city matches God. Therefore, the last time the Bible mentions man, it says that man as God's counterpart matches God. When the Bible first mentions man, it says that man bears the image of God, but when the Bible mentions man at the end, it says that man is God's counterpart. This shows us that God is working continuously for the purpose of working Himself into man to make man one entity with Him. The first step of this work was the incarnation of the Lord Jesus. When the Lord was incarnated, He was called Emmanuel, which means "God with us" (Matt. 1:23).

There are two aspects of God's being with man. God was

not only among men, but He also came into man. When the Lord Jesus was in the flesh, He was with the disciples, but this kind of presence was not sufficient. It was objective and outward, not inward. Therefore, one day the Lord Jesus told the disciples that He was going to the Father who had sent Him. This made the disciples sorrowful. Then He told them that it was expedient for them that He go away, because if He went, He would come again (John 16:5-8). Before He went away, He was with the disciples by being in their midst, but when He came back, He would be with the disciples by being in them.

GOD MINGLING WITH MAN

In the evening of the Lord Jesus' resurrection, He came into the midst of the disciples and breathed Himself into them, saying, "Receive the Holy Spirit" (20:22). This was an extremely great matter. From that time on, the Lord Jesus dwelt in His disciples. He was not bound by time or space; for instance, the Lord was able to enter into the midst of the disciples even though the doors were shut (v. 19), and after He talked with the two disciples who were going to Emmaus and reclined at table with them, He suddenly disappeared from them (Luke 24:30-31). Thus, we must see that from the day of the Lord Jesus' resurrection, His presence with the disciples progressed from being merely outward to being inward, from being visible to being invisible, and from being limited by time and space to being outside of time and space.

In John 20 the Lord breathed into the disciples (v. 22). This fulfilled what He had spoken earlier: "In that day you will know that I am in My Father, and you in Me, and I in you" (14:20). This was also the fulfillment of what He had prayed to the Father concerning being in the disciples—"that they may be perfected into one, that the world may know that You have sent Me and have loved them even as You have loved Me" (17:23). The Gospel of John mentions several "in"s. Chapter fourteen verse 10 reveals that the Father is in the Lord. When Philip asked the Lord, "Lord, show us the Father and it is sufficient for us" (v. 8), the Lord answered, "Have I been so long a time with you, and you have not known Me?" (v. 9).

Outwardly the Lord was a Nazarene, but inwardly He was the Father. God was in Him. Not only was the Father in the Lord, but in verse 20 we see that on the day of resurrection the disciples would know that the Lord was also in the Father. The Lord is in the Father, we are in the Lord, and the Lord is also in us. On the day of resurrection, the disciples saw and realized these three "in"s. These three "in"s tell us that God, we, and Christ are mingled as one entity.

When the Lord came to the earth, He entered, with God, into man in order to be united with man as one. Hence, Romans 8 clearly reveals that Christ's being in man is not only God's being in man but also the Spirit of God's being in man (vv. 9-10). Then Ephesians 3 shows us that Christ makes His home in our hearts through faith that we may be filled unto all the fullness of God (vv. 17-19). When all the fullness of the Godhead dwells in us bodily, we will be one with God completely. God's purpose in us is to work Himself into us. We have to ask God to open our eyes that one day we would see this. This is the first vision in the Bible, and this is also the first vision concerning the relationship between God and us.

ALL OF GOD'S WORK BEING
TO WORK HIMSELF INTO MAN

God created us as His vessels so that He could put Himself into us. God also redeemed us for the purpose of working Himself into us. Suppose a house is built for us. If the inside of the house is not too messy, we can simply move in, but if it is messy, then we must put things in order before we can move in. If man had not fallen or been corrupted, God could have simply moved into him, but because man became corrupted and fallen, he needed redemption. Redemption was the clearing procedure God used to make us clean and tidy so that He could come live in us. God was also gracious to us in causing us to believe in Him and be saved so that He could enter into us. Our confessing, repenting, keeping morning watch, reading the Bible, praying, listening to messages, and attending special edifying meetings are for the purpose of allowing God to come into us further. We need to see this great vision.

GOD COMING INTO MAN
IN ORDER TO GAIN A DWELLING PLACE

The purpose of God's work in man is this one thing—to work Himself into man. He desires to dwell in man, to be joined to man as one, and to take man as His dwelling place. This is God's work in us. If we repent, yet we do not have God dwelling in us, our repentance is futile. If we confess, yet we do not have God dwelling in us, our confession is in vain. In the same way, if we do not have God dwelling in us in our morning watch, our morning watch means nothing. If God does not enter into us in our Bible reading, our Bible reading is worthless. If God does not enter into us in our prayer, our prayer has no value. If we attend a meeting, yet God does not enter into us in that meeting, that meeting is meaningless. If we listen to messages and attend special meetings, yet God does not enter into us, all of these things are futile. The most important matter in our Christian life is that God would be brought into us so that He would enter into us to gain a dwelling place. Everything is for this purpose. All our activities, whether preaching the gospel, repenting, confessing, or pursuing the Lord, are for the purpose of allowing God to enter into us to gain the dwelling place He desires.

THE WAY FOR GOD TO MINGLE WITH MAN

The Bible reveals that the crucial matter in the relationship between God and man is that God wants to work Himself into man, and the way this purpose is accomplished is through His mingling with man. First Corinthians 6:17 says, "But he who is joined to the Lord is one spirit." Our being joined to the Lord as one spirit means that God is joined to us in our spirit. God is Spirit, and He also created a spirit for us. The reason God created a spirit for us is so that we would have an organ to receive Him. Only our spirit can receive the Spirit of God, which is God Himself.

If man had only a mind, emotion, and will but not a spirit, he would have no way to contact and receive God. This is why the more a rational and intelligent person thinks, the more he feels that there is no God. After pondering over this matter very much, many highly educated people say that there is no

God. They do not realize that we cannot contact God in our mind. We can contact God only in our spirit. Whenever we disregard our mind, ignore our thoughts, and use our deepest part to touch God and to pray to God, we are filled with God. The more we pray, the more we are filled with God, and the more we pray, the more we have the presence of God.

I hope that all of us would see that God's presence with man is not in his soul—his mind, emotion, and will—but in his spirit. It is only in the spirit that man can be joined to God as one spirit. Our spirit is our innermost part where we may contact God and mingle with God. When we see the vision of the mingling of God and man, we will have the way to be mingled with God. May God be gracious to us that we may despise all other matters and simply seek to be joined and mingled with God in spirit.

QUESTIONS, ANSWERS, AND TESTIMONIES

Question: One time shortly after I had been saved, I was at home feeling very depressed within. Because I felt so depressed, I asked the church to pray for me. Then I met a brother on the road. After I had fellowship with him, I felt much better, but after I walked ten or twenty steps farther, the inner feeling came back again. Why did that happen?

First, we must be clear about the way of experience. When you have a feeling, you should not immediately go to fellowship. Rather, you should shut your door and pray to God wholeheartedly from deep within. You may say, "O God, I feel very depressed within. Please come to relieve my depression." After you pray, you must discern what your inner condition is and then decide whether or not you should go to a brother for fellowship. If you do not pray before you go to other people for fellowship, your inner being certainly will not be satisfied. Every feeling of depression within us is a call for us to pray to God. If we still have the feeling of depression after praying, then we should go to the brothers for fellowship.

Testimony: When I was young, I did not obey my parents, but after being saved, the Lord enlightened me and showed me my flesh. I even quit smoking and drinking. Not only so, before I was saved, I had a bad temper, but the Lord has been dealing with me little by little. This is how I have changed since the Spirit of God entered into me. I have received God, and He fills, regulates, keeps, and comforts me.

We all have to learn to touch the presence of God from our innermost part in silence. The dealings between God and man are the dealings of the Spirit with our spirit. God is Spirit, and He created a spirit for us that we may contact and receive Him. From the day of our salvation, we should learn not to pay attention to our mind, emotion, and will but to exercise our spirit to contact God and to allow the Spirit of God to come into us. This is the fellowship of the Spirit with our spirit, the echo of the Spirit in our spirit, and the feeling of the Spirit in our spirit. In this way our spirit will be strengthened, bright, and living. Because our spirit is strengthened, bright, and living, its demand will spontaneously increase, and our dealings with God in spirit will also increase and broaden. Hence, we all must learn to touch the feeling of the spirit from our deepest part.

Testimony: I have had many failures, particularly in my experience concerning this matter of our being joined to God in the spirit. It is very hard for God to reign in me because most of the things I like are frustrating to the spirit. I am one who has fallen deeply in my mind, emotion, and will. I long to be delivered from this, but practically it is not that easy. I have been trying to submit to the spirit, but I have failed every time. My wife just gave birth to our fifth child, so basically I have no way to attend the meetings. However, inwardly I felt that this kind of thinking was out of the flesh, and I had no peace in my heart, so I came. I put my self aside. May the Lord have a free way in me.

This kind of experience is very precious and accurate. It clearly shows us how our mind, emotion, and will need to cooperate with the spirit. Many times we do not touch the feeling of our spirit. Our will is unyielding, and our emotion and mind are not cooperative. We must realize that God's work of breaking and tearing down in us who have received mercy is to deal with our mind, emotion, and will. He wants us to be subdued. Hence, as long as we have a feeling in our spirit, we should ignore what we are thinking in our mind, what we are feeling in our emotion, and what we are deciding in our will. Those who are able to ignore their mind, emotion, and will are those who have been strongly enlightened by God, smitten by God, broken by God, and torn down by God. If we set our heart on God and desire that He would gain the ground in us, we have to be prepared for Him to strongly shine on us and smite us with His hand sooner or later.

Our mind, emotion, and will need to cooperate with the spirit. When we pursue God, He works in our spirit and requires us to submit to the ruling of the spirit and the demand of the spirit. When we meet a person who has much spiritual experience and who knows how to touch the spirit, we will find that he is not thoughtless, having no mind. Rather, his mind is spiritual. Although his mind is not the spirit, his mind is in submission to the spirit. We will also find that we can touch his emotion. He can easily sympathize with people, being full of love, yet we will find that his emotion is also controlled by the spirit. As for his will, he may be very strong, but once he touches the spirit, he is submissive. We may say that he has a strong but spiritual will. This kind of person is truly a spiritual man. We need this kind of spiritual reality so that our mind, emotion, and will may all be subdued to live under the spirit.

Question: How can we tend toward the center? In one of her books, Madame Guyon talks about a tendency toward the center. One who tends toward the center can see that he is opposing God, and after he has tended toward the center, he will confess and repent outwardly. What is it to tend toward the center?

This question is actually a question of what and where the human spirit is. We have said before that the spirit of man is man's innermost part. For us to allow the Lord to mingle with our inner man, our spirit, we first need to see that it is useless for us to only know teachings. We may have heard the teaching of living in the spirit several times, even to the point where we are able to speak it to people. But if we remain unchanged and continue to do things the way we used to do them, this teaching will not profit us. One day the Holy Spirit will give us the light and open our inner eyes to show us that

the most important matter in the universe is that God wants
to mingle Himself with us. From that time on, something
within us will move us and change our direction. Then we will
learn to touch the presence of God and to fellowship with
God, and we will clearly realize that the dealings between
God and man are in the spirit.

The dealings between God and man occur in a place deeper
than man's mind, emotion, and will. They occur deep in man's
spirit. Sometimes the dealing is silent, and at other times it is
vocal. Sometimes it is without form, and at other times it
is with a form. Sometimes it is an explicit word, and at other
times it is merely a groaning. In such a way we learn to fellowship with the Lord, not in our mind but deep in our spirit.
We begin to realize that the demand in our spirit is something
that our will cannot subdue, our emotion cannot answer, and
our mind cannot agree with. Our innermost being is in a
certain condition whereas our soul is in another condition. It
is as if we are two men, living a life of contradiction.

Many times within us there is a demand, yet our will
refuses to submit to it, our mind does not incline toward it,
and our emotion does not like it. Conversely, sometimes there
is an inclination in our mind, emotion, and will, but our innermost part, our spirit, has no peace. At times like these we find
that we are divided people. On the one hand, we are in the
spirit while, on the other hand, we are in the soul. Moreover,
our spirit is in conflict with our soul, which means that God is
in conflict with us. The spirit represents God while the soul
represents man. If we tell God, "God, I want You, and I choose
to be on Your side," then the Holy Spirit will break forth from
our spirit. Once our heart chooses God and stands on God's
side, the Holy Spirit breaks forth from our spirit. However, do
not think that the Holy Spirit is that strong. Many times the
Holy Spirit is not as strong as our will. This is why many
people, even though they have been moved by the Holy Spirit
numerous times, still refuse to repent and believe in the Lord.

Sometimes the Holy Spirit is able to break forth from
within us, but because our mind, emotion, and will are too
strong, even the Holy Spirit cannot conquer us. Because of
this, God's hand arranges an appropriate environment to

smite our being. God knows that it is only through endless smiting that our mind, emotion, and will can be subdued and controlled by the spirit. I hope that from now on in our fellowship meetings or daily conversations we would all rid ourselves of fellowshipping about blessing and peace, or matters such as receiving healing from sickness and prospering in business. Rather, we should share our testimonies of submitting to the spirit. Through this kind of mutual encouragement, everyone will desire to live in the spirit and enter into a deeper union with the Lord.

However, we must remember that merely listening to messages will not help us to have these experiences. We need the Spirit of God to open our eyes that we may see this, know this, and live in it. To receive more exhortations and doctrines is useless. After hearing the messages, the Spirit of God must one day open our eyes to show us that the unique way in this universe that God wants to take in us is to mingle Himself with our spirit. When we see this, our inner being will turn, and we will have a longing and prayer from within. At that time, we will reconsecrate ourselves. We will say to God, "God, here I am—a person who has received Your mercy, whose eyes have been opened to see the way that You desire to take. God, I am willing to answer this revelation, this calling, to surrender my mind, emotion, and will into Your hands. From now on I will no longer struggle in my mind, emotion, and will. I desire to yield to You my entire being." This consecration is a different kind of consecration, a renewed consecration.

This is the first vision concerning the relationship between God and man. The first vision those who pursue and serve the Lord must see is that God wants to enter into man. To merely see that we are sinners is too shallow, and to merely see that our sins have been forgiven is too superficial. We must see that God's intention is to come into us and that within us we have a spirit as a vessel to receive Him. From the time we see this vision, we will surrender to Him. Then we will be joined to Him in our spirit and will no longer live in our mind, emotion, and will but in our spirit.

CHAPTER TWELVE

THE TWO PRINCIPLES OF CHRIST

Romans 8:9 says that since the Spirit of God dwells in us, we are in the spirit, and therefore, we are of Christ. Philippians 3:10 says, "To know Him [Christ] and the power of His resurrection." This verse implies that only by knowing the power of resurrection can we know Christ. In 2 Corinthians 5:16 Paul said, "So then we, from now on, know no one according to the flesh." Even though the apostle had known Christ according to the flesh, he no longer knew Christ in that way. The apostle Paul confessed that before his salvation he had known Christ according to the flesh, not according to the spirit, but now he knew Him so no longer.

In the Bible we see two principles that are related to Christ. One is the principle of incarnation, and the other is the principle of death and resurrection. Only when we know the principles of incarnation and of death and resurrection can we know Christ in a thorough way. If we do not know what incarnation and what death and resurrection are, our knowledge of Christ will be strictly doctrinal and will not have much impact on us. Only by knowing these two principles of incarnation and of death and resurrection can our knowledge of Christ be of life, not of doctrines, and be subjective, not merely objective.

THE PRINCIPLE OF INCARNATION

What is the principle of incarnation? The principle of incarnation is God coming into man. This is something that is truly of the Spirit and that requires the Holy Spirit to thoroughly shine in us so that it may become our inward vision. The incarnation of the Lord is to bring God into man. Before the Lord Jesus was born, God could not enter into man because He had not been incarnated. God's entering into man began with the incarnation of the Lord Jesus. Hence, in the Old Testament there was no such thing as God entering into man because at that time incarnation had not yet begun, and God and man had not yet been mingled together.

Incarnation began with the birth of the Lord Jesus, but did incarnation stop at that time? The answer is no. Not only was the birth of the Lord Jesus incarnation, but every time someone is saved, that is also incarnation. When you and I repented and believed in the Lord, we received the Lord Jesus into us. That was incarnation happening once again.

The birth of the Lord Jesus was the beginning of incarnation in the universe. Since that time, incarnation has been occurring again and again, time after time, and day after day. Ever since the birth of the Lord Jesus, which was the first time God came into man, there have been many other times in which God has come into man. What is the story of our salvation? Our salvation is the story of God coming into man. Every person's salvation is a story of God coming into man. This is the principle of incarnation.

Therefore, we need to see that the first principle concerning Christ is incarnation—God coming into man. Do we have this principle in us? Are we incarnated people? The fact is that all of us saved ones have this principle in us. Through our believing in Him and receiving Him, the Lord Jesus entered into us. Thus, we became incarnated people. Strictly speaking, those who have not passed through incarnation have not been saved. Hence, we have to say from our heart, "Thank and praise the Lord! The principle of incarnation that is in Christ is also in us." Incarnation is God coming into man. As those who have been saved, God has come into us. We all have the story of incarnation on us and in us.

THE PRINCIPLE OF DEATH AND RESURRECTION

The second principle concerning Christ is the principle of death and resurrection. What is the meaning of death and resurrection? Incarnation is God entering into man, and death and resurrection are man entering into God. If we want to know Christ, we have to know these two principles. Christ is God entering into man, and Christ is also man entering into God. God entering into man and man entering into God are the two principles concerning Christ, the two stories of Christ. Everything that Christ went through is included in these two principles. Through incarnation, He as God came into man to become man. Then through death and resurrection, He entered into God again. Through incarnation and through death and resurrection, He accomplished and passed through what He had to accomplish and pass through. These two principles embody everything that relates to Christ and also what God is doing throughout the ages. The work that God wants to do is to work Himself into man and man into Himself, so that God and man, man and God, would be mingled as one.

We all have the principle of incarnation in us, but do we have the principle of death and resurrection? As saved ones we all have God mingled with us, and we have the assurance to say that God has entered into us and is touching us all the time. We also can testify to people that we have God in us and that God is dwelling in us. In 1936 I was living in Tientsin, and one day I was praying in my room, preparing to give a message on the Holy Spirit's dwelling in us. After I prayed, I had the feeling that it was so glorious to have God dwelling in me. I wanted to run through the streets, telling everyone that I had a wonderful person—God—in me.

All the saved ones have the feeling that God is in them, but some may have a weaker feeling, and others may have a stronger feeling. Every genuinely saved person has a mysterious story in him. Even though he may not be able to explain it, within him there is a mystery, a story, which only he himself is able to feel. This mystery is that God is in him. Thus, every saved one has the principle of incarnation. However, Christ has more than just the principle of incarnation within Him. In Christ there is not just a one-way traffic but a two-way traffic, a coming and a going. Christ came in His incarnation, and He went in His death and resurrection. His coming is God's entering into man, and His going is man's entering into God. His coming is His incarnation, and His going is

His death and resurrection. Therefore, when we remember
the Lord at the Lord's table, we have to praise the Lord that
He not only came through incarnation but also went through
death and resurrection.

"COMING" AND "GOING"

In preaching the gospel, most people speak much about
the Lord's coming but not about His going. The Lord Jesus
Himself said, "But I tell you the truth, It is expedient for you
that I go away; for if I do not go away, the Comforter will not
come to you; but if I go, I will send Him to you" (John 16:7).
When the Lord mentioned His coming, He simply touched on
it lightly. He said that the Son of Man had come to seek and to
save that which was lost (Luke 19:10). When He mentioned
His going, however, He stressed it very much. The Lord's
going was expedient for us. If He had not gone, the Holy Spirit
would not have come. In John 14, 15, and 16, the word *going* is
very significant. The Lord Jesus is not only the Lord who
came but also the Lord who went. His coming was His incarnation, and His going was His death and resurrection.

We already know that we all have the principle of
"coming," that is, the principle of incarnation in us, but do we
have the principle of "going"? Do we have the principle of
death and resurrection in us? The principle of death and
resurrection is to bring man to the heavens, to bring man into
God. The Lord has now come into us, and His life has passed
through death and resurrection. Thus, the One who dwells in
us is the God of death and resurrection. When we are joined
to Him, we are joined to His death and resurrection, so we
also have the principle of death and resurrection. Objectively,
we have died and were resurrected, but subjectively, we have
not completely died and been resurrected.

EXPERIENCING THE PRINCIPLE OF
DEATH AND RESURRECTION

According to the objective aspect, when Christ died and
was resurrected, we also died and were resurrected. But
according to the subjective aspect, we seldom have the experience of death and resurrection. When we were saved, the

principle of incarnation took place in us, and God truly dwelt in us. Now all of our experiences, history, and progress should be in the principle of death and resurrection. The principle of incarnation took place in us when we were saved, but now all of our spiritual experiences, history, and progress hinge on the principle of death and resurrection.

Every saved one experienced regeneration when God entered into him. What is regeneration? Regeneration is God coming into man. Thus, incarnation already took place in us in our salvation. From the time of our salvation, our experience, progress, and spiritual story depend on the principle of death and resurrection. Hence, the story of a Christian is exactly the same as the story of Christ. The stories of Christ are the stories of incarnation and of death and resurrection, that is, the stories of God entering into man and man entering into God. These are also our stories—the stories of incarnation and of death and resurrection, of God entering into man and man entering into God.

What are death and resurrection? Death and resurrection are man's entering into God. All of our experiences after salvation are to bring us into God. So what does it mean to have "death" in us? We have already said that for us to know Christ, we must know His death and resurrection and the power of His resurrection. All that Christ had was brought through death—His mind, His emotion, His will, His actions, and even the life of God in Him were brought through death. Everything that He had was brought into death to pass through death. With us, the principle is the same. Everything that we have must be brought through death. If you say that you have the principle of death and resurrection, then I would ask you if everything you have has been brought into death. Has everything you have passed through death? Some people may be deep in their experience of this whereas others may be more superficial. Some may experience this principle in a partial way whereas others may experience it in many ways. Regardless of how we experience this, none of us have fully passed through death. Not until we are raptured will we have fully passed through death and resurrection.

We need to know Christ according to these two principles.

In His incarnation He brought God into man, and through His death and resurrection He brought man into God. All of us saved ones have some experience of incarnation because we have God in us. However, we still need to experience death and resurrection. We need the experience of our mind, emotion, will, and everything being brought into death and passing through death so that through the principles of incarnation and of death and resurrection we may have a living knowledge of Christ, a knowledge which is subjective and of life.

CHAPTER THIRTEEN

DEATH AND RESURRECTION

(1)

Scripture Reading: Rom. 8:9-11; Eph. 1:19-23; Phil. 3:10

THE MINGLING OF DIVINITY AND HUMANITY

There are two great principles concerning Christ. One is incarnation, and the other is death and resurrection. These two principles include everything that Christ experienced. Through His incarnation He brought God into man, and through His death and resurrection He brought man into God. This coming and going accomplished God's work of mingling Himself with man, and as a result, God was able to gain a man in this universe. This man is not a natural man but one who has God mingled with Him and has passed through death and resurrection. This man is a God-man, a man who is the mingling of God and man, and a man of resurrection. This man enabled God to gain a model, a standard, in the universe.

In Christ we can fully see both the divine element and the human element. These two elements, however, do not exist separately from each other. God is no longer merely God, and man is no longer merely man, but God and man have been mingled together. Through His death and resurrection Christ brought man completely into God, just as His incarnation brought God completely into man. Through His incarnation and through death and resurrection, God and man, man and God, were fully mingled as one. The God who is in Christ is a man-God, and the man who is in Christ is a God-man. His divinity contains humanity, and His humanity contains divinity. As a result of Christ's resurrection, divinity and humanity are no longer separated but are mingled together.

The mingling of divinity and humanity is the purpose of God's plan in eternity. In the Scriptures we see that the one thing God desired from eternity past was to mingle His nature with the human nature so that He and man would no longer be separated. The accomplishment of this mingling required two procedures. The first is incarnation, and the second is death and resurrection. Through incarnation and through death and resurrection, divinity and humanity were mingled as one. Hence, in the Lord Jesus Christ we see the result that God desired—the mingling of divinity with humanity.

The goal that God has been intending to achieve through-out the ages and the purpose of His choosing, predestinating, redeeming, edifying, building, leading, and being gracious to us is to work Himself into us and, at the same time, to completely work us into Himself. In other words, the purpose of all of God's work is to work divinity into humanity and humanity into divinity, that divinity and humanity would become fully one. Through this, God will be able to obtain what He is after in the universe. Apart from divinity and humanity, God has no other goal. God has no intention to obtain some other result in His work. What God desires to obtain is divinity and humanity, that is, to work divinity into humanity and humanity into divinity, that the two would be fully mingled as one and that divinity would be in humanity and humanity in divinity.

THE PROCEDURE OF THE MINGLING OF GOD AND MAN

Today this goal has not yet been accomplished in us. Thus, the new heaven and new earth and the New Jerusalem have not yet appeared. Hence, what God wants to do in us is to work His nature into us and our nature into Him more and more. This procedure or process involves a "coming" and a "going." The coming is His incarnation, and the going is His death and resurrection. The principle of incarnation is God coming into man to be mingled with man, and the principle of death and resurrection is man going into God to be mingled with God. From the day of our salvation, God's work in us has been to bring our humanity into divinity, to bring us into God.

THE PRINCIPLE OF DEATH AND RESURRECTION

The principle of death and resurrection is to bring man into God. It is incorrect, however, to say that a person who has passed through death and resurrection is absolutely devoid of the human element, having only the divine element. A person who has passed through death and resurrection is one who has been mingled with God. His human element has not been nullified. Rather, it has been mingled with the divine element. The incarnation of the Lord Jesus was God coming into man, God putting on man. He put on man, passed through death, and entered into resurrection, and in His death and resurrection He brought the man that He had put on into resurrection. Then what is resurrection? Resurrection is the sphere or realm of God. The Lord Jesus died and resurrected, and through His death and resurrection He brought the man that He had put on into the realm of God.

We need the light and the revelation of the Holy Spirit to see these matters of incarnation and of death and resurrection. Our natural mind has no way to fully comprehend this matter of God coming into man and man coming into God, and our words are not adequate to express it. This mystery of God being man and man being God does not exist in our human mind. It is beyond our human thought and concept. To see this matter requires the revelation of the Holy Spirit.

THE INCARNATION OF THE LORD JESUS— GOD COMING TO BE A MAN

While Jesus the Nazarene was living on the earth, did He live as a man or as God? The Bible tells us that while the Lord Jesus was on the earth, He lived as a man, not as God. In the Gospels the Lord told people again and again who the "Son of Man" was (Luke 6:5) and what the "Son of Man" had come for (9:56). By this He indicated that He was the Son of Man. The Lord Jesus rarely revealed His status as God. Instead, He always lived out His condition as a man. Only once, when He was transfigured on the mountain, did He fully manifest the condition of God within Him before the disciples. Aside from that instance, we can say that He seldom revealed His condition as God. In the thirty-three and a half years He was on the earth, He mostly lived out His condition as a man. He was a man living on the earth. However, He lived out His humanity by His divinity. He was God living the life of a man.

You and I are humans, and the life that we live is one hundred percent a human living. What is a human living? What is the means by which we live out our human living? A human living is a living that a man lives out spontaneously and effortlessly by his humanity. For example, I am a Chinese, my nature is Chinese, and it is natural for me to have a Chinese living. It is not difficult at all for me to have a Chinese living according to the Chinese nature. While the Lord Jesus was on the earth, the life He lived was exactly the same as ours, except that He was without sin. However, did He live by His humanity or by His divinity? He lived a human life by His divinity. Most of us live out the human life by our humanity, but because He was God coming into man, our Lord lived a human life by His divinity.

While the Lord Jesus was on the earth, His living was apparently the same as that of Peter and John. Just as Peter and John lived out the human life, so also the Lord Jesus lived out the human life. Outwardly speaking, they all lived the human life, but Peter and John lived the human life by man, while the Lord Jesus lived the human life by God. They all lived the human life, but Peter and John lived a human life as men, and Jesus the Nazarene lived a human life as God. In Peter and John's living, there was the flavor of man but not the flavor of God. The living of Jesus the Nazarene, however, was full of the flavor of God. Outwardly He had the form of man, but inwardly His content had the element, nature, and flavor of God.

Although the Lord lived a human life on the earth, He spontaneously expressed His divinity and manifested His divine nature. Why was this the case? It was because He was actually God. His divinity had been put into a man and was constrained, pressed, and confined by this man. He was great, even infinitely great, but He limited His infinite greatness to a small man. Thus, the life that the Lord lived on the earth was that of a man in appearance but was actually God in its content. God was concealed in a man. He intentionally lived a human life by His divinity so that He might mingle His divinity with humanity. This is the principle of incarnation.

THE DEATH AND RESURRECTION OF THE LORD JESUS— MAN COMING TO LIVE GOD

In His death and resurrection the Lord Jesus did not put off the humanity that had restricted, bound, and limited Him. Since the purpose of His incarnation was to bring God into man, and His goal was ultimately to bring man into God, it was not possible for Him to put off His humanity. In His death and resurrection He did not put off His humanity. Rather, He brought the humanity that He had put on into God. In His incarnation the man that He put on was finite and limited, but in His death and resurrection He brought the man whom He still had on into death. In resurrection this man was transfigured. Before His resurrection this man had been finite, but through His death and resurrection this man became infinite. Formerly He had been a man, a finite man, but through His death and resurrection, this finite man was brought into the realm of resurrection and entered into God. Thus, He became infinite. Through death and resurrection the man who was finite became infinite.

God is infinite and eternal, but the man the Lord Jesus put on, before entering into death, was a finite and limited man. After the Lord Jesus passed through death and entered into resurrection, the man He had put on became eternal and infinite. Because He entered into God, what was finite became infinite, and what was temporal became eternal. Through death and resurrection this man fully entered into God and was mingled with God. In the thirty-three and a half years that the Lord Jesus was on the earth before His death and resurrection, He lived a human life that was filled with divinity inwardly and that expressed God spontaneously, and after His resurrection when He appeared to His disciples, what He expressed was God's living. Romans 1:4 says that in

His resurrection, He "was designated the Son of God in power."

In His incarnation the Lord Jesus appeared as the Son of Man, but after His death and resurrection He appeared as the Son of God. In His incarnation He appeared as a man in the midst of men, but after His resurrection He appeared as God among men. As God, the Lord Jesus was incarnated to live a human life, but He died and resurrected to live God's life. Just as He lived a human life that was different from man's living, so also He lived God's life in a way that was different from God's living. This statement may seem too extreme, but the fact is that when He was on the earth, although He lived a human life, He was different from ordinary men. Similarly, after His resurrection, although He lived God's life, He was different from the God before incarnation, death, and resurrection.

Before the Lord Jesus was incarnated, He was already God. After His death and resurrection He again expressed Himself as God. However, the God whom He expressed at that time was very different from the God whom He had expressed before incarnation. What was the difference? The difference was that before His incarnation He as God did not have humanity, but after His incarnation He as God possessed humanity and was full of humanity. When the Lord Jesus was on the earth, He lived a human life in which the divinity that was in Him was expressed spontaneously. In like manner, after His resurrection what was expressed was God's living, but it was a living in which the humanity that filled Him was also expressed spontaneously.

Death and resurrection did not put off or nullify man. Instead, death and resurrection brought man into God, causing man to become the content of God. Hence, incarnation is God becoming the content of man, and death and resurrection are man becoming the content of God. Incarnation is for God to become man to live out a human life while death and resurrection are for man to become God to live out God's life.

DEATH AND RESURRECTION NOT NULLIFYING MAN

When we truly know death and resurrection, many things

will happen to us. We all know that all the Epistles written by Peter, John, Paul, and James are parts of the Word of God. However, when we read the Epistles of Paul, we find that the flavor of Paul's Epistles is absolutely different from that of Peter's Epistles, and the flavor of the Epistles of John is altogether different from the flavor of the Epistle of James. What each of them wrote was the Word of God, but when we read the Epistles of John, we sense John's flavor, when we read the Epistles of Peter, we sense Peter's flavor, when we read the Epistle of James, we sense James' flavor, and when we read the Epistles of Paul, we sense Paul's flavor. All of their writings are the Word of God, but the flavors are not the same. Why is this? It is because of death and resurrection. Death and resurrection do not nullify man but bring man into God. Hence, Paul's speaking was God's speaking, Peter's speaking was God's speaking, James' speaking was God's speaking, and John's speaking was God's speaking. Through death and resurrection they entered into God and were mingled with God. They were not nullified or done away with. Rather, they still existed.

People of death and resurrection are not without their own mind, emotion, and will. Rather, their will is strong, they are thoughtful, intelligent, and wise, and they are the most emotional people, easily angered or easily made to rejoice. Do not think that it is unspiritual to be angry. Many Christians have the concept that spiritual people are always meek. They think that no matter how much spiritual people are irritated, they will not lose their temper. If being meek is spiritual, then the statues of Mary in the Catholic Church must be the most spiritual. Recall that even the Lord Jesus became angry, and His rebukes were harsh. He rebuked the scribes and Pharisees, saying, "Serpents! Brood of vipers!" (Matt. 23:33) and "You resemble whitewashed graves" (v. 27). One day He entered into the temple of God and cast out all those who were selling and buying in the temple (21:12). Seemingly, He was not reasonable, overturning the tables of the money-changers and the seats of those who were selling doves. Our Lord was full of wrath. Paul also had a similar story. He said to the Corinthians, "What do you want? Should I come to you with a rod or in love and a spirit of meekness?" (1 Cor. 4:21). Therefore, a spiritual person is not devoid of emotion. In fact, the more spiritual a person is, the more emotional he is. To be spiritual is not to be nullified or done away with. Genuine spirituality is the issue of death and resurrection. The principle of death and resurrection is the bringing of man into God.

According to the principle of death and resurrection we have been brought into God, yet we still exist. In the past we were not in God, nor did we have the element of God, but now we are in God and have the element of God. We still have our mind, but we also have God's mind in us. We still have our will, but we also have God's will in us. We still have emotions, but we also have God's emotions in us. God's emotions are in our emotions, God's mind is in our mind, and God's will is in our will.

I have a very heavy burden within me regarding this matter. Most of God's children have heard many messages and have much in the way of knowledge and doctrines but have not touched this reality. They speak of the spiritual doctrines concerning death and resurrection, such as nullifying the self, denying the self, and being delivered from the self. This kind of speaking is useful only when it serves the purpose of mingling us with God, that is, mingling our mind, emotion, and will with God. Otherwise, all we have is empty knowledge and doctrines. Incarnation brings God into man, producing the living out of a human life by the divinity of God. Death and resurrection bring man into God, producing the living out of God's life through the humanity of man.

Most of those who have read the Bible know that the Epistles of Paul are full of Paul's flavor, while the Epistles of Peter are full of Peter's flavor. From this we see that God does not nullify man. Just as the twelve tribes of Israel will still be the twelve tribes in eternity future, the twelve apostles of the New Testament will still exist as the twelve apostles in eternity future. Even after entering into the new creation, man will not be nullified. Instead, God will be mingled with man. Formerly God was God, having no humanity mingled with Him, and man was man, having no God in him. But now divinity has been mingled with humanity, and man has God in him. In the past, man did not have God, and what had been added into man was sin, Satan, and the world. Now due to Christ's redemption all of these things have been taken away, and the element of God has been added into us.

Hence, before we were saved, we all sinned, but when we were saved, God was added into us, and as a result we are no longer slaves of sin. Nevertheless, we are not nullified. Though all of us have had God added into us, our lives still have different flavors because we as men have not been nullified. Peter had the flavor of Peter, John had the flavor of John, James had the flavor of James, Paul had the flavor of Paul, and you have your flavor, and I have my flavor. God has come in, but man has not been nullified.

THE PERSONALITY OF MAN STILL EXISTING AFTER EXPERIENCING DEATH AND RESURRECTION

Death and resurrection do not put man aside or nullify man but bring man into God. In eternity future God will see many different faces with many different personalities and kinds of humanity joined as one in His divinity. Everyone will live out God Himself, but each one will do so with his own flavor and character. In eternity, in the last poem of God, we will see that the brothers will have the brothers' flavor, but at the same time they will all have the glory of God, and the sisters will have the sisters' flavor, but at the same time they will also have the glory of God. This is death and resurrection. Death and resurrection do not mean that we no longer exist but that we enter into God.

It is terrible to be a person without humanity, and it is terrible to be a Christian without humanity. It is right to be humble, but to be humble without humanity is not right. It is right to be meek, but to be meek without humanity is not right. It is right to give hospitality, but to give hospitality without humanity is not right. This means that a person should not be too mild. Even mud should bear the flavor of mud. If a person becomes so spiritual that even his human flavor is gone, then he must be pretending. Such a one is full of the flavor of falsehood, and his understanding of death and resurrection is wrong.

Sadly, this kind of spiritual pretense and falsehood exists among Christians today. For example, there was once a sister, who, pretending to be spiritual, lowered her shoulders, bent her waist a little, took a few seconds to sit down, and then remained still. People were amazed when they looked at her. However, was this sister spiritual? No, she was just pretending. Her self and natural man had not yet been broken. Instead, they were deeply hidden in her.

Genuine spirituality is reached through death and resurrection. Man is not nullified or done away with. Rather, man is still there, but this man has entered into God. In the past, regardless of whether we were sinful or not sinful, good or bad, we did not have the element of God in us. Now we not only have been cleansed from our sin, but we also have God in us. Thus, if we could have seen James, we would have seen God; if we could have seen Peter, we would have seen God; and if we could have seen Paul, we would have seen God. Their "human flavors" were not nullified but were brought into God.

Through death and resurrection man enters into God and is mingled with God. Death and resurrection do not mean that there is no longer man and that there is only God. If this were the case, then in eternity there would only be God Himself and no man. God keeps on working because He has no intention to nullify man. Hence, we should not be influenced by the erroneous doctrine that we should pretend in any way. If we are influenced in this way, eventually we will lose our human flavor. If there is a brother among us who is quick and stubborn, we should never try to annul his quickness and stubbornness, because this will cause him to become like mud or tofu. What he needs is to pass through death and resurrection. He may be quick and stubborn as an ox, and no one may be able to do anything with him. However, after passing through death and resurrection, his stubbornness may still be there, but there will be the flavor of God in his stubbornness. His stubbornness will be in God and will have the element of God. Likewise, he may still be quick, but his quickness will be in God and will have the element of God.

One who is in God still has his own personality and existence, but he has entered into God. This is what God is doing.

One day we will all see a beautiful scene in which there will be all kinds of people with various characteristics in all the churches, yet all of them will have entered into God, will be living in God, and will have the flavor and glory of God. This will not only be a beautiful scene but also a beautiful song. What a glory it will be to Him when all of us different people are in our great God and are living out His image and His flavor! This is what God wants. This is death and resurrection.

SPIRITUAL REALITY BEING MAN PLUS GOD

Just as incarnation brings God into man to live a human life with the flavor of God, so death and resurrection bring man into God to live God's life with the existence of man. In this way, God is in man, man is in God, and both God and man share one living.

Therefore, on the one hand, while we need to have our own personality, on the other hand we all have to learn to allow the Holy Spirit to bring our personality into God. We have no need to imitate other people. In the past several thousands of years there have not been two saints who were the same. Many Christians want to imitate Madame Guyon in her piety and spirituality, but Madame Guyon was Madame Guyon, and no one can look like her by imitation. God has no intention to nullify us, and we have no way to imitate others. The sixty-six books in the Bible were written by more than forty people. Even though all the books are the Word of God, the Pentateuch has the flavor of Moses, the book of Isaiah has the flavor of Isaiah, the book of Jeremiah has the flavor of Jeremiah, and the book of Daniel has the flavor of Daniel. It was impossible for one to imitate the other.

We should be spiritually influenced by others, but we should not imitate them. No one can utterly put himself aside and imitate others. We should not even imitate the Lord Jesus. The Lord wants us to deny ourselves and to enter into Him. He does not want us to live in ourselves. If there were no man in the universe, God would feel the emptiness the most. If there were no man in the universe, God's work would equal zero. Hence, what God is after is that all of us who are different would enter into Him and mingle with Him. God has no intention to nullify us. Therefore, the more a person is in resurrection, the more human he will be. The more a person is in resurrection, the more he will have humanity and the stronger his humanity will be.

In death and resurrection, it is not that man is nullified or done away with. Rather, when man reaches the realm of resurrection he looks more human, is more human, and has more human flavor, having human thoughts, emotions, and will. However, all of these are mingled with God. Formerly all of these did not have the element of God, but now they all are mingled with God. May God have mercy on us to show us that spiritual reality is not the nullification of ourselves. Rather, spiritual reality is man plus God so that man may live God's life in God. Though it is God's life, it is full of human flavor. Just as God came to be a man to live a human life that was full of God's flavor without nullifying the human flavor, similarly, we also should be full of humanity while we are living God's life. Our humanity should not be nullified. Instead, we should be more human and even be men above all men.

CHAPTER FOURTEEN

DEATH AND RESURRECTION

(2)

Scripture Reading: John 7:39; Acts 2:32-33; Rom. 1:4; John 11:25; 2 Cor. 3:17

THE CROSS BEING THE LORD'S DEATH

Incarnation brings God into man, and death and resurrection bring man into God. It is easy for people to comprehend that incarnation is God's coming to be a man, but most people do not truly understand the matter of death and resurrection. What is death, and what is resurrection? Death is the cross. Every time we mention the Lord's death, we understand it to mean the Lord's crucifixion. The cross of the Lord is His death. Whenever we experience the Lord's death, we experience the Lord's cross. In other words, without the cross there is no death of the Lord. Where there is the Lord's cross, there is the Lord's death, and whoever has the Lord's death has the Lord's cross. When we speak of experiencing the Lord's death, we imply the experience of the Lord's cross. The experience of the cross is the experience of death.

THE HOLY SPIRIT
BEING THE LORD'S RESURRECTION

We may already have a clear and accurate knowledge regarding the Lord's death, but we still may not comprehend or be able to explain the Lord's resurrection. In John 11 the Lord said to Martha in person, "I am the resurrection and the life" (v. 25). This word tells us that the Lord Himself is the resurrection and that resurrection is the Lord. However, the Lord's flesh was not the resurrection, and thus, He had to pass through the cross. Before passing through the cross, He was in the flesh; after passing through the cross and entering into resurrection, He became the Spirit (1 Cor. 15:45b; 2 Cor. 3:17).

The Lord's flesh was not the resurrection, but when He became the Spirit, His whole being became the resurrection. Hence, the Lord's being the resurrection today implies His being the Spirit. If He were not the Spirit, He would not be the resurrection. In other words, resurrection is the Spirit, and the Spirit is the reality of resurrection. Apart from the Spirit there is no reality of resurrection.

John 7:39 says, "For the Spirit was not yet, because Jesus had not yet been glorified." The glorification of Jesus was His resurrection. In the resurrection of the Lord Jesus, He became the Spirit. The Spirit is the embodiment of resurrection. This means that resurrection is wrapped up in the Holy Spirit and embodied in the Holy Spirit. In other words, the resurrection of the Lord Jesus is realized in the Holy Spirit. Everything of resurrection is in the Holy Spirit. In Acts 2:32-33 Peter said, "This Jesus God has raised up, of which we all are witnesses. Therefore having been exalted to the right hand of God and having received the promise of the Holy Spirit from the Father, He has poured out this which you both see and hear." This indicates that after the Lord Jesus resurrected and received the Holy Spirit from God, He poured out the Holy Spirit.

Everything of resurrection is in the Holy Spirit, and everything that is in resurrection can come into us in the Holy Spirit. In the Lord's resurrection, all the things in resurrection come into us through the Holy Spirit. In John 14:2 the Lord said that He had to go. This meant that He had to go to suffer death. Then He said that He would come again (v. 3). His coming again was His resurrection. His going was His death, and His coming was His resurrection. However, His coming again was as the Holy Spirit. His going was His death, and His coming again was His resurrection as the Spirit. His coming as the Holy Spirit was His coming in resurrection. He brought resurrection into the Holy Spirit, and He Himself is the resurrection.

Verse 19 says, "Yet a little while and the world beholds Me no longer, but you behold Me; because I live, you also shall live." The two instances of the word *live* in this verse convey the story of resurrection. After the Lord's resurrection He came into us as the Holy Spirit. He is living in resurrection, and because He lives in us, we live, and we also live in resurrection. The Lord's resurrection is altogether realized in the Holy Spirit, and the resurrected Lord is the Holy Spirit. Apart from the Holy Spirit, there is no resurrected Lord, and similarly, apart from the Holy Spirit, there is no realization of the resurrection of the Lord. The resurrected Lord and the Lord's resurrection are both in the Holy Spirit. When we touch the cross, we touch death, but when we touch the Holy Spirit, we touch resurrection. Hence, the cross is the Lord's death, and the Holy Spirit is the Lord's resurrection.

THE LAMB STANDING AS HAVING JUST BEEN SLAIN, SIGNIFYING THE LORD'S RESURRECTION

In Revelation 4 and 5 we see two pictures. The first picture is of a throne, and upon the throne there is One sitting. There are also seven lamps of fire before the throne, which are the seven Spirits of God, the Holy Spirit (4:2, 5). The second picture shows us that in the midst of the throne and of the seven Spirits before the throne there is a Lamb standing as having just been slain (5:6). The phrase *having just been slain* refers to death, and *standing* refers to resurrection. The Lamb standing as having just been slain signifies that He not only died but that He lives again. Revelation 5 shows us that the Lamb who was slain and resurrected is the Christ who died and resurrected.

The seven Spirits before the throne are the seven lamps of fire. Why are they lamps of fire? It is because God is a consuming fire, and from the God of consuming fire comes fire. In order that we would not be afraid, God put this fire in a lamp. The fire is the Spirit because God is Spirit. The Spirit is God, and the fire also is God, so the Spirit is the fire. Thus, on the day of Pentecost, the Holy Spirit was poured out as fire.

God is the Spirit and the fire, the fire and the Spirit, because what comes out of God are Spirit and fire. This is what we see in Revelation 4. Then in chapter five there is a Lamb in the midst of the throne and of the four living creatures, and this Lamb has seven eyes, which are the seven Spirits of God. Originally, the seven Spirits of God were the seven lamps of God, but after Christ's death and resurrection, the seven Spirits of God became Christ's seven eyes.

In Revelation 4 the Spirit of God is the seven lamps of God that enlighten the universe. But in chapter five the Lamb who was slain is standing, indicating that He has died, resurrected, and ascended. Before Christ's death and resurrection, the Spirit of God was the seven lamps of God. After Christ's death and resurrection, the Spirit of God became Christ's seven eyes, which observe the whole universe, the whole earth. The seven eyes are the seven Spirits of God, being sent forth into all the earth. The seven eyes of Christ observe the whole earth. Wherever Christ's eyes look, His Spirit reaches, His light shines, and His fire burns.

CHRIST AS THE RESURRECTED LAMB
CONTACTING MAN AS THE HOLY SPIRIT

Revelation 4—5 shows us the scene of Christ's ascension. After Christ passed through death, resurrection, and then ascension, He stood in the midst of the throne and the four living creatures. He was the resurrected Lamb, and He was resurrection. There was a Lamb standing before the throne in heaven. This standing Lamb was resurrection. Resurrection hinged on Him, depended on Him, and was in Him. However, where did Christ, the resurrected Lamb, put Himself so that He could be contacted and received by man? The resurrected Christ put Himself into man and became the Holy Spirit so that man could contact and receive Him.

We have seen that everything of resurrection is in the Holy Spirit. Christ is the resurrection and the totality of resurrection. Resurrection is in Him, He is resurrection, and He is now the Holy Spirit for man to contact and receive. In other words, the reason why the Christ who is in the heavens can reach the earth and be contacted and received by man is that in resurrection He put Himself into the seven Spirits, and He is diffused through the seven eyes. The seven eyes are the seven Spirits of God, and the seven Spirits are the Holy Spirit. The number seven implies completion. In Revelation the number seven describes the function of the Holy Spirit, indicating that the function of the Holy Spirit is complete. He is well able to satisfy all our needs both great and small.

Therefore, the resurrected and ascended Christ has become the Holy Spirit, and through the Holy Spirit He looks at man's inner being and comes into man. Through the Holy Spirit, He contacts man, has fellowship with man, and is received by man. Suppose a brother is standing at a distance from you. If he wanted to contact you, how would he reach you? First, he would look at you with his eyes. When your vision and his vision join together, even though there may be a distance between you and him, the distance is bridged through your eye contact. The Holy Spirit is the eyes that diffuse and shine forth Christ. Wherever the Holy Spirit looks, Christ shines, and wherever the Holy Spirit shines, Christ reaches. In addition, whomever the Holy Spirit looks into, Christ shines into, and whomever Christ shines into, that one has fellowship and contact with Christ inwardly.

THE HOLY SPIRIT BEING
THE REALITY OF RESURRECTION

As the Holy Spirit, the resurrected and ascended Christ came to the earth to contact man, to be touched by man, to fellowship with man, and to be received by man. The resurrected and ascended Christ is resurrection. Resurrection is in Him, and He became the Holy Spirit. Hence, the Holy Spirit is resurrection. If we want to touch resurrection, we must touch the Holy Spirit. Everything of resurrection is realized in the Holy Spirit. Whenever we touch the Holy Spirit, we touch resurrection. Just as there is no death apart from the cross, there is also no resurrection apart from the Holy Spirit. Only when we touch and experience the cross will we touch and experience death. Only when we touch and experience the Holy Spirit will we touch and experience resurrection.

Due to the lack of light, in the past we thought we knew

about resurrection, when actually we did not know about it. Now, however, we know that resurrection is in the Holy Spirit and that the Holy Spirit is resurrection. The Holy Spirit who was poured out after Christ's ascension is resurrection. The resurrected Christ ascended to the heavens. He is the totality of resurrection, and everything of resurrection has been gathered into Him.

In the Gospel of John, the Lord not only said that He was the resurrection but also that He had to ascend to heaven and come back as the Holy Spirit (14:26, 28). When He comes back as the Holy Spirit, He shines on us and looks at our inner being. The Holy Spirit is resurrection. In other words, resurrection is in the Holy Spirit. The Holy Spirit is connected to resurrection, and resurrection is contained in the Holy Spirit. What is in the Holy Spirit is resurrection. This may be likened to a glass containing grape juice. Wherever the glass is placed, the grape juice is there. Resurrection is contained in the Holy Spirit. Wherever the Holy Spirit is, there is resurrection. There is no resurrection outside of the Holy Spirit. The Holy Spirit is resurrection. Our experience can prove this. Every time we are in resurrection, we are living in the Holy Spirit. In the same way, every time we live in the Holy Spirit, we are living in resurrection. When we are living in our natural life, we are living in our self and the flesh, but when we are living in the Holy Spirit, we are living in the resurrected Lord. When we receive Christ's death, we receive Christ's cross, and when we live in the Holy Spirit, we live in resurrection.

In short, the Lord's death is the cross, that is, the Lord's cross is death, and the Lord's Spirit is resurrection. Before the Lord's resurrection, the Holy Spirit was not available as resurrection, but now after the Lord's death and resurrection, everything of resurrection is in the Lord, and the Lord is in the Holy Spirit. Thus, resurrection is in the Holy Spirit. Just as the cross is the reality of the Lord's death, so also the Holy Spirit has become the reality of resurrection. Where there is the cross, there is death, and likewise, where there is the Holy Spirit, there is resurrection. Without knowing the Holy Spirit, our talk about resurrection is vain, because the Holy Spirit is the reality of resurrection.

THE APPLICATION OF
THE LORD'S DEATH AND RESURRECTION

To experience the Lord's death, we must receive the cross. We must see that when the Lord was nailed to the cross, we also were hung on the cross. We have already been crucified and dealt with. If a person wants to experience the death of the cross, he must see and receive the cross. Similarly, if a person wants to experience resurrection, he must see that when Christ was resurrected and ascended, He put everything of resurrection in the Holy Spirit. The Holy Spirit as the embodiment of the resurrected Christ is the descending of the glorified and resurrected Christ.

The Holy Spirit of Pentecost is the embodiment of the resurrected Christ. The resurrected Christ is the Holy Spirit. The Holy Spirit wants to enter into us, but how can He do this? A sinner is saved because he has an experience of the Holy Spirit. At the beginning he may feel that God is visiting him and that God's eyes are looking at him. He may immediately feel that he is a sinner, even a worthless sinner, yet God is willing to visit him with His own eyes. This look is God's eyes. This is the story of the embodiment of the Spirit of God in us. This look is the first step. Then the second step is enlightenment. After He looks at us, our inner being is enlightened. Once He enlightens us, we immediately feel that we are very filthy and corrupted. Whether a person is a sinner or a saint, when he experiences the Holy Spirit, the principle is the same. When God's eyes look at us, we are immediately enlightened by the Holy Spirit. The third step is the burning of the Holy Spirit. Eventually, the Holy Spirit enters into us, and we experience the Holy Spirit.

In other words, God is embodied in Christ, and Christ is realized as the Holy Spirit. When the Holy Spirit enters into us, we then live in the Holy Spirit. God first looks at us, and then He enlightens us. Once He has enlightened us, He burns us, and once He burns us, we live in the Holy Spirit. When we are living in the Holy Spirit, we are living in resurrection. At this time, our inward feeling is the feeling of the Holy Spirit, the feeling of resurrection, and our inward power is the power of the Holy Spirit, the power of resurrection. Hence, the power of resurrection is the Holy Spirit. Romans 8 calls the Holy Spirit "the Spirit of the One who raised Jesus from the dead," indicating that the Holy Spirit is the Spirit of the One who raised Jesus from the dead (v. 11). The power of the resurrection of the Lord Jesus is the Holy Spirit. His resurrection was accomplished through the power of the Holy Spirit. The power is the Holy Spirit, and the Holy Spirit is the power of resurrection. We are touching the reality that the Holy Spirit has entered into us. The Holy Spirit is the power of resurrection and is resurrection. After He looks at us, He enlightens us; after He enlightens us, He burns us; and after He burns us, the Holy Spirit comes into us. He is resurrection.

Now we have an inward power which enables us to overcome the world, sin, and Satan, to bear what is unbearable, to suffer persecution, or to be martyred. This power is what 2 Corinthians 4 calls the excellency of the power (v. 7). In us earthen vessels there is an exceedingly great power that is of God and not of us. This exceedingly great power in us enables us to be pressed on every side but not constricted and to be cast down but not destroyed (vv. 8-9). This resurrection power is the Holy Spirit, the resurrection, which is in us, who are vessels. This power enables us to live a life of holiness, not fearing hardship or suffering. Today we can be conformed to Christ's death because we know the power of His resurrection in us.

We know that God is the Spirit. When the Spirit of God touches our spirit and interacts with our spirit, there is spiritual reality. Christ is this spiritual reality. Not only so, the Spirit of God is the seven Spirits of God, the seven lamps of God, and the seven eyes of God. When the seven eyes look at our inner being, they shine into our inner being. When they shine into our inner being, they burn in our inner being, and eventually, the Spirit comes into our spirit to be our spiritual reality. Hence, we see that the Holy Spirit is everything. God is the Holy Spirit, Christ is the Holy Spirit, resurrection is the Holy Spirit, power is the Holy Spirit, and resurrection life is also the Holy Spirit. When the Holy Spirit touches our spirit, contacts our spirit, and meets with our spirit, there is an issue—spiritual reality.

We can see in Revelation 4 that the ascended Lamb looks at our inner being through His seven eyes and that these seven eyes are the seven eyes of God. He looks at our inner being, enlightens our inner being, and burns in our inner being. Thus, we live in the reality of resurrection and in the power of resurrection. Then this reality and power lead us to have a kind of living that we cannot live by ourselves. This living is in resurrection and by the power of resurrection.

QUESTIONS AND ANSWERS

Question: After Christ was resurrected, He could no longer die, yet with us, we live in the Holy Spirit one day but live in the flesh another day. Does this mean that resurrection can be changed in our experience? Why is it that incarnation is once for all, but God's work in us is in the principle of death and resurrection? What does this mean?

Answer: After being resurrected, the Lord Jesus cannot die again but lives forever. However, in our experience, we may not live in resurrection continuously. Our experience of death and resurrection may last for only one day or only half a day before we turn back to our flesh. When this happens, we need to die again. Most of us stay in the Holy Spirit for a very short period of time and then leave. This is very real. Hence, in terms of our experience, we do not have a solution to this problem, because in this age we still have the flesh and the old creation in us. This is why we always say that a Christian is a dual person, having a dual condition. This dual condition cannot be resolved until we are raptured and delivered from the old creation and the flesh. At that time in eternity, we will live in resurrection in reality and will never go back.

Presently, our flesh and old creation are with us. Therefore, we need to experience the death of the cross every day. Every time we experience death and live in the Holy Spirit, we enter into resurrection, but when we do not live in the Holy Spirit, we are not living in resurrection. When we turn back and live in the flesh and the self, we immediately sense that we should live in resurrection. At that time we need to pass through death again. In brief, most of us may be living in our self, our soul, being motivated and directed by our mind, emotion, and will. However, the cross requires us to put our mind, emotion, and will to death. By this, we deny our soul, our self, and turn back to our spirit. Then we are in the Holy Spirit, in resurrection and then our mind, emotion, and will are brought into our spirit. This is to bring man into God, to pass through death and enter into resurrection. Then our spirit within, that is, the Spirit of God, will direct our mind, emotion, and will from our soul. We will be living in the Holy Spirit, in resurrection.

Sometimes we leave the realm of resurrection as soon as we wake up from our sleep. Our mind thinks by itself, our emotion loves by itself, and our will makes decisions by itself, and as a result we live in our flesh. However, through fellowship and prayer, we may enter into resurrection and allow God to direct our being. This condition is very normal and spiritual because we have been mingled with and joined to God. In this situation the Spirit of God reigns in us and dominates us, directing our mind, emotion, and will in order to bring our spirit under the ruling of the Spirit of God. This is resurrection.

For example, we may wake up in the morning with our own ideas, and with them come our mind and emotion. We may neglect our spirit and turn back to the self. At such a time we are going backward and are not in the Holy Spirit. After we suffer a blow and encounter some difficulties, we may be enlightened and turn back. In other words, we may pass through death and enter into resurrection again. This experience is repeated in us continuously. We may wish to stay in the spirit all the time, but most of the time we enter into the spirit and then leave it again. Sometimes we go in and out several times a day. When we kneel down to pray, we enter into the spirit, but when we rise up and contact people, we leave our spirit again. We may quickly get out of our spirit and just as quickly enter into our spirit. This is very normal. However, the most normal situation is that once we enter into our spirit, we remain there all the time. This is what the Lord desires.

The incarnation of Christ took place in us once at the time

we were saved. After we are saved, all of our experience is in the principle of death and resurrection. Incarnation is God coming into us. This took place in us when we were saved. Each one of us experienced the principle of incarnation at that time, and there is no need to repeat it. After that time, what matters is the principle of death and resurrection. The principle that we must apply in our work, our service, our living, and our experience is not incarnation but death and resurrection. Incarnation was accomplished in us once for all. All of God's riches came into us on the day of our salvation. But our entering into God depends on our experience of God after our salvation. God's work in us is to bring us into Him through death and resurrection. The final step of death and resurrection is our rapture in transfiguration. The principle of rapture in transfiguration is still death and resurrection, that is, to enter fully and completely into God.

Question: If we say that God saves us that He may live in us, then what is the purpose of reading the Bible and praying?

Answer: The purpose of all our activities—whether reading the Bible, praying, meeting, or preaching the gospel—is for God to live in us. At the time of our salvation, we received all of God's riches, but now the big question is how to know and experience these riches. After we are saved, we receive God by coming to the meetings, reading the Bible, and praying, but this does not mean that we receive more than what we received at the time of our salvation. Rather, it is through reading the Bible, praying, attending meetings, preaching the gospel, and our daily living that we know and experience what we have received. On the day of our salvation, everything of God entered into us, and we cannot receive more than that. In our experience, however, we may know, experience, or enjoy only a little of what we have received. We have already received the riches, but when we have more experiences, then we will have the feeling of being filled with all of God's riches.

Question: In our experience, the Holy Spirit comes out through our soul, but if our soul is blocked, will our soul restrict the work of the Holy Spirit in us?

Answer: The coming out of the Holy Spirit from within us is not affected by us. The Holy Spirit Himself is exactly the same, being no different, regardless of whom He comes out of. However, the Holy Spirit does not nullify us but mingles us into Him and thus comes out from us. Due to the differences in each one of us, the results of this mingling in each one of us are not the same. The Holy Spirit Himself is the same in all of us, but His mingling with us varies from person to person. The result of this mingling is different for each one of us.

Paul, Peter, John, and James all wrote parts of the Bible, but Paul's writing bears Paul's flavor, Peter's writing bears Peter's flavor, John's writing bears John's flavor, and James' writing bears James' flavor. All these writings are the Word of God and the moving of the Holy Spirit, and all of them came out of the Holy Spirit. However, because they were written through man's cooperation and man's mingling with the Holy Spirit, the four of them are different and have their own flavor. The reason is that man's personality is not nullified in the mingling of the Holy Spirit. Rather, it still exists.

Question: How do we discern our soul from our spirit?

Answer: In order to see the distinction between the soul and the spirit, we must realize that the soul is the mind, emotion, and will. Every time we live and walk by our mind, emotion, and will, we are living by and in our soul. One who pursues the Lord should not be like this. He should not live directly by his mind, emotion, and will. Rather, he should turn to his innermost part and take care of the sense deep within his being.

The deepest sense within us is from the spirit. There is a sense in our innermost part that comes from the spirit and represents the spirit. We should allow this sense to direct our mind, emotion, and will so that they do not take the first place but the second place in our living. In other words, our spirit should have the first place in our living, directing our soul—our mind, emotion, and will. In short, our soul is the totality of our mind, emotion, and will, and our spirit is the sense of our innermost part. It is enough to know the spirit and the soul in this simple way. Do not try to analyze. The more we analyze, the more confused we will be.

Question: When we were saved, God's light came in, and

*we received the Holy Spirit. Why do we still need to be enlight-
ened again?*

Answer: When we were saved, the Spirit of God looked at
us and shined into us, and at that point the Holy Spirit
entered into us. But after our salvation, God's eyes still look
at us continuously, again and again, from the outside in and
from the inside out. Sometimes we sense that the heavenly
eyes are looking at us, and other times we sense that He is
looking from within us. This is the fellowship of the Holy
Spirit. Fellowship is not a one-way traffic. Christ is in the
heavens, and He is also on the earth. He is in us, and He
is also outside of us. Because He is the Holy Spirit, Christ is
omnipresent. Sometimes He comes to us from the heavens,
and sometimes He comes from within us. These comings and
goings are for us to touch His presence and thus increase our
experience of Him.

*Question: Concerning the experience of death and resurrec-
tion, how is man's personality brought into God through the
Spirit of God? Does it involve getting rid of the old creation in
Adam?*

Answer: This question, in fact, does not require any analysis because the more you analyze, the more confusion there
will be. We must hold on firmly to the principle that death
and resurrection have already brought us into God. However,
one thing is certain—all our defilement, sins, worldliness, and
corrupted nature cannot be brought into resurrection. Before
we enter into resurrection, we must pass through the cleansing of the precious blood and the dealings, and what remains
after that is the man before the fall, the man originally
created by God, which can be brought into God. Therefore,
before we can be raptured in transfiguration, we must enter
into God, which depends on the cooperation of our mind, emotion, and will with the Holy Spirit.

God transforms us by mingling our mind, emotion, and
will with the Holy Spirit, so that the entire organ of our soul
is controlled and directed by the Holy Spirit. Our mind must
be mingled with the Holy Spirit, our emotion—our joy, anger,
sorrow, and delight—must be mingled with the Holy Spirit,
and our will must also be mingled with the Holy Spirit. Our

entire living must issue from the mingling of the inward
organ of our soul with the Holy Spirit. Our body, however,
will not be brought into God's glory until the day that we are
raptured. On that day, our body will be brought into glory.

When God's life comes into us, transformation begins.
Then throughout our entire lifetime, He has to change the
body of our humiliation into the body of His glory, from being
finite into being infinite, from being weak into being strong,
and from being temporal into being eternal. Romans 8 says
that we will enter into the freedom of the glory of the children
of God (v. 21). We have to enter into a realm that is free and
belongs to the glory of God.

Today our body is still full of limitations, but when our
body is fully transfigured, we will enter into the glory of God,
and there we will be free from any limitation. Before the
transfiguration of our body, we already have the Spirit of
God in our spirit. Our spirit has already been regenerated.
Now the Spirit of God needs to enter into our soul to control
and direct our soul. In this way the organ of our soul will be
transformed. Originally, our soul was merely our mind, emotion, and will, but now our soul is being mingled with the
Spirit of God. Our mind, emotion, and will are becoming spirit.
Eventually, we will have a spiritual mind, a spiritual emotion,
and a spiritual will, and what we live out will be something
spiritual—spiritual reality.

When the Holy Spirit first comes into our spirit, our spirit
is regenerated. This is the first step of the working of the
Holy Spirit in us, and this is in the realm of the spirit. After
we are saved, God requires us to submit to His Spirit. This
submission includes putting our mind, emotion, and will under
the ruling of the Holy Spirit so that our entire soul becomes
the sphere for the work and operation of the Holy Spirit. The
Holy Spirit operates in us to direct our whole soul—our mind,
emotion, and will. Eventually, our whole soul will become the
sphere for the work and operation of the Holy Spirit.

When we proceed and become more spiritual, the power
of the Holy Spirit will permeate our mind, emotion, and will
and direct our body, so that it will be changed—our weakness
will be made strong, and our sickness will be healed. Romans 8

says that He will give life to our mortal bodies (v. 11). At that time, our body will also become the sphere for the operation of the Holy Spirit. However, it is not until we are raptured that the Holy Spirit will operate in our entire body, causing our body to be changed into a glorious body. At that time, our whole being will be the sphere of the operation of the Holy Spirit. Thus, we see that in our experience of the process of death, resurrection, and transfiguration, the sequence is first the spirit, then the soul, and then the body.

Question: It is easy for our emotion to submit to the Holy Spirit, but it is not that easy for our mind to submit. What shall we do?

Answer: If it is easy for your emotion and will to submit to the Holy Spirit but not your mind, this may be your own particular problem. In brief, the meaning of having our mind, emotion, and will ruled by the Holy Spirit is to not allow our mind, emotion, and will to have the preeminence. You have to consider whether a certain matter comes from your mind or from the feeling of your spirit. If it comes merely from your mind, you have to stop it, but if it comes from the feeling of your spirit, you have to submit to it. This is to have your mind under the ruling of the spirit. In speaking about this we may analyze in this way, but in our practical experience we should never analyze, because too much analysis is not healthy. You have to learn not to live in your mind, emotion, and will but in the feeling of your spirit. Just bear this principle in mind, and do not analyze too much.

Question: How does the Holy Spirit direct our mind and emotion?

Answer: This kind of question is dangerous because it may bring us into analysis. Please remember that we cannot live directly and simply in our mind, emotion, and will. We have to allow our spirit to rule over our mind, emotion, and will. For instance, you may want to love a brother, but this may be just the reaction of your emotion. Therefore, you should not love him right away, but you should ask whether or not your spirit agrees with you. Does your innermost part allow you to do this or not? Once you ask, you will be able to know. If it is you making the decision, this is the activity of your soul, and you have to stop it immediately. You have to wait until there is the motivation in your spirit for you to love that brother, and then your emotion has to cooperate with it.

Sometimes your spirit may require you to love a brother, but your emotion does not prefer him. In such a situation, would you say that your emotion is under the direction of your spirit? If there is another brother whom you like in your emotion, but your spirit forbids you to like him, will you listen to your spirit? Your emotion may be like metal and that brother like a magnet that attracts the metal. What can you do? Regarding the first brother, your spirit requires you to use your emotion, but you are not willing to do so. Regarding the second brother, your spirit forbids you within and does not allow you to use your emotion, but you choose to. This shows what the activity of the emotion is and what the ruling of the Holy Spirit is. If you learn to love the Lord, live in the spirit, and put aside your own emotion, you will not do things directly and simply from your emotion but from your spirit, and your emotion will cooperate. The mind and will also function in the same principle.

CHAPTER FIFTEEN

EXPERIENCING DEATH AND RESURRECTION

Scripture Reading: Matt. 22:31-32; 1 Cor. 15:4-5, 8-11; 2 Cor. 4:7-11; Phil. 3:10; Eph. 1:19-23

THE SPIRIT OF GOD IN THE OLD TESTAMENT HAVING NO ELEMENT OF HUMANITY OR RESURRECTION

Resurrection is not something objective and vague, because resurrection is the Holy Spirit, and the Holy Spirit is the reality of resurrection. After the Lord's resurrection and ascension, the Holy Spirit, in which is resurrection, was poured out. Now the Holy Spirit is the Spirit of resurrection. We all know that in the Old Testament the Spirit was not yet the Spirit of resurrection. After the Lord's resurrection and ascension, the Holy Spirit was outpoured from heaven. It was then that the Holy Spirit came as the Spirit of resurrection. The Holy Spirit today is very different from the Spirit in the Old Testament.

In the Old Testament the Spirit had only the divinity of God but not the humanity of man. After the Lord's death, resurrection, and ascension, the Holy Spirit descended from the resurrected Christ in the heavens. This Holy Spirit who descended not only had the divinity of God but also the humanity of man. In the Old Testament the Spirit had not yet passed through the process of death and resurrection. However, after the Lord's resurrection and ascension, the Holy Spirit descended from heaven, having passed through death and resurrection. Now the Holy Spirit has two additional elements—humanity and resurrection.

Hence, in the Old Testament the Spirit of God had neither

the humanity of man nor the element of resurrection mingled with Him, because Christ had not yet been incarnated and had not passed through the process of death and resurrection. God had not yet been mingled with humanity, and humanity had not yet been mingled with God. Thus, at that time the Spirit of God had only the divine element of God, not the human element of man or the element of resurrection.

THE HOLY SPIRIT OF GOD BEING GOD HIMSELF

The Bible clearly says that God is Spirit (John 4:24). This means that Spirit is the essence of God, the nature of God. For instance, suppose we have a wooden table. We can say that the table is wood because the table is made of wood. God is Spirit. Hence, the Holy Spirit of God is God Himself. Never think that God is merely God, the Holy Spirit of God is merely the Holy Spirit of God, and the two are separate. We can say that the table is the table, and we can also say that the table is wood because the essence of the table is wood. Likewise, the Spirit of God is God Himself because God's nature, God's essence, and God Himself are Spirit. The Holy Spirit is God Himself, and no one can separate the Holy Spirit from God. Sadly, some people in Christianity make the mistake of separating the Holy Spirit from God. They reason that if the Holy Spirit and God were one entity, not two, then God could not have sent the Holy Spirit. If the Holy Spirit and God were one, then God would have sent Himself. Actually, it is true that God sent Himself.

We must realize that the hidden God is God but that the expressed God is the Spirit. The God who dwells in unapproachable light is God, but every time He comes out, He is the Spirit. There is a hidden place in heaven that man cannot approach. The Bible calls it unapproachable light (1 Tim. 6:16). That place is much more severe than the furnace of fire in Daniel 3, where men were slain even at a distance from it. God dwells in unapproachable light. In this unapproachable light He is God, but when He comes out, He is the Spirit. In Genesis 1 when God came out to create all things, He was the Spirit. There it says, "The Spirit of God was brooding upon the surface of the waters" (v. 2).

Every time God wants to speak through man, He comes as the Spirit of God. The Spirit of God and God Himself are not two separate entities but one. If we think of the Spirit of God and God Himself as two separate persons, we will never be clear about spiritual matters and spiritual reality. For us to have spiritual experiences and reality, we must clearly see that the Holy Spirit is God Himself. God in heaven is God, but when He comes to us, He is the Spirit. He is not two but one. The Spirit of God is God Himself.

THE HOLY SPIRIT BRINGING FIVE ELEMENTS TO US

In the Old Testament God had not yet been incarnated and had not yet passed through death and resurrection. Thus, when the Spirit of God came out in the Old Testament, He did not have the elements of humanity and resurrection. He did not have the elements of death and resurrection. In other words, the Spirit in the Old Testament age was solely the Spirit of God, not the Spirit of death and resurrection. The elements of humanity and resurrection were not in Him. Then in the New Testament the Word became flesh. The Bible records that the birth of the Lord Jesus was due to the Holy Spirit's entering into Mary. When God is in heaven, He is God, but when He comes out, He is the Spirit. God is also the Word (John 1:1). The Word becoming flesh is God who is the Spirit becoming flesh. At that time the Spirit entered into man.

When God became flesh, He put on man, bore man, and added humanity. After His death and resurrection He went back, bringing humanity into heaven and into God. Thus, in His death and resurrection the elements of death and resurrection were added into Him. After His ascension He descended as the Spirit and came upon man.

In the Old Testament the Spirit of God came upon man directly from God, but the Spirit who came upon man possessed only the element of divinity, not the elements of humanity and resurrection. Then in the New Testament age God became flesh, died, resurrected, ascended, and descended as the Spirit upon man. At that time the Spirit of God had the elements of humanity and resurrection. Before God became flesh, the

Spirit of God was merely the Spirit of God, lacking the human element. One day, however, God came out, entered into man to become flesh, passed through death and resurrection, brought man into Him, ascended to heaven, and descended from heaven. Consequently, the Spirit of God now has the divinity of God, the humanity of man, and the elements of death, resurrection, and ascension. Today the Holy Spirit who comes into us has the elements of death, resurrection, and ascension. This is so mysterious!

After the Lord's resurrection and ascension, the Holy Spirit descended. Many Christians do not understand this. They think that the Holy Spirit after the Lord's resurrection and ascension is the same as the Spirit in the Old Testament age. Before the incarnation of the Lord Jesus, God was in heaven, and He was simply God. But now after the Lord's incarnation, death, resurrection, and ascension, this One who is in heaven is not that simple. He is no longer merely God but a God-man. He is God who put on humanity. He is altogether different from what He was before His incarnation. Before His incarnation He was merely God. But because of His incarnation, death, resurrection, and ascension, He now has other elements in Him and is no longer merely God but a God-man. In the same way, we saved ones had merely the human element before we were saved, but once we were saved, the divine element was added into us, and we became God-men.

Since we have the principle of incarnation in us and are God-men, our inward constitution is not that simple. It is not so simple because we have another element—the divine element. God has the human element added into Him whereas man has the divine element added into him. In this way the two—God and man, man and God—are mingled as one. In the Old Testament age the Spirit was simple, but in the New Testament age the Holy Spirit is not that simple. In the Old Testament age the Spirit was simply the Spirit of God, lacking the human element and not having passed through death, resurrection, and ascension. But in the New Testament age the Holy Spirit possesses the divine element and also the human element.

Before incarnation, whenever the Spirit came upon man,

He came only with the divine element. Now having passed through incarnation, death, resurrection, and ascension, the Holy Spirit brings with Him five elements—God, man, death, resurrection, and ascension. The Holy Spirit who came upon Mary possessed only the element of divinity, but the Holy Spirit who was already in Peter by the time of Pentecost had five elements.

THE HOLY SPIRIT ENTERING INTO MAN
WITH ALL THE RICHES OF GOD

We have already seen that resurrection is the Holy Spirit, the Holy Spirit bears resurrection, resurrection is in the Holy Spirit, and ascension is also in the Holy Spirit. After we are saved, we may read the Bible and various spiritual publications. As a result, we may see that we have been resurrected together with Christ and are ascended together with Christ. However, for many years after our salvation, we may live merely in this empty doctrine because we may only believe and say what the Bible says. We may say, "Amen, that is right. We have been resurrected together with Christ and are ascended together with Christ." But as far as our experience is concerned, we have not been resurrected or ascended. One day, however, the Lord will show us that resurrection and ascension are in the Holy Spirit. Where the Holy Spirit is, there is resurrection and ascension. When the Holy Spirit comes into us, resurrection and ascension also come into us.

Today the question is not whether we have ascended to the heavens but whether the Holy Spirit has entered into us. Today it is not a matter of us having to die, to be resurrected, and to ascend to the heavens. Rather, it is a matter of death, resurrection, and ascension already being in the Holy Spirit. Everything that God has, has passed through, and has attained are all in the Holy Spirit. The Holy Spirit is so rich.

Do we realize this? Do we believe this? We may have been Christians for many years but may still think that the cross is merely the cross, the Holy Spirit is merely the Holy Spirit, and the two are not related. One day, however, God will open our eyes to show us that the Holy Spirit is very rich. All the riches of God are in the Holy Spirit. The Holy Spirit who dwells in us today is so rich. Not only is all that God has in the Holy Spirit, but all that God has passed through and attained are also in the Holy Spirit. Apart from the Holy Spirit there is no cross, no resurrection, and no ascension in our experience. Death, resurrection, and ascension are all in the Holy Spirit. Only by knowing the Holy Spirit in such a way are we able to experience His riches.

Where is God? Where is God's power? Where is God's character? Where is all that God has done? Where is incarnation? Where is Christ? Where is the death of the cross? Where is resurrection? Where is ascension? Where is holiness? Where is the revelation of God? Where is the enlightenment of God? Where is the anointing of God? Where is the Word of God? Where is the vision of God? There is only one answer—in the Holy Spirit. It is impossible to find something that God has, is, has passed through, has accomplished, or has attained that is not in the Holy Spirit. The Holy Spirit is so great and so rich!

TO LIVE IN THE HOLY SPIRIT BEING
TO LIVE IN RESURRECTION

When I was young, I knew that God was triune, but my concept was that the Father was the highest, the Son was lower, and the Spirit was the lowest. The Father, the Son, and the Spirit are equal, but in our understanding we usually arrange them in order of the Father, the Son, and the Spirit, thinking that the Son is lower than the Father and that the Spirit is lower than the Son. Many people think that the Father, the Son, and the Spirit are like stairs. The Father is the first step, the Son is the second, and the Spirit is the third. We must see that the Father is in the Spirit and that the Son is also in the Spirit. Thus, when we touch the Spirit, we touch the Father, and when we touch the Spirit, we touch Christ the Son. If we are not experiencing the death of the cross, we are not living in the Spirit, because the death of the cross is in the Spirit. Where there is the reality of the Spirit, there is the death of the cross. Today if we do not have the reality of resurrection in us, this indicates that we are not in the Spirit and that we have lost the fellowship of the Spirit, because the element of resurrection is in the Spirit. When we touch the Spirit, we touch resurrection.

We are those who live on the earth, but whenever we live in our spirit, we sense that we are in the third heavens, living a heavenly life on the earth. However, whenever we live in the flesh and in ourselves, we immediately feel that we are crawling on the earth and that we are earthy, full of earthly feelings. Once we are filled with the Holy Spirit and live in the Holy Spirit, we will sense that we are living in the heavens. We will sense that we have ascended to the third heavens and that we are heavenly. Although we are still living on the earth, inwardly speaking, we may already be in the heavens. It is not we who have ascended to the heavens, but it is the heavens that have come into us, because the heavens are in the Holy Spirit. When the Holy Spirit comes, He comes with God, incarnation, death, resurrection, and ascension. All of these items have entered into us in the Holy Spirit.

Now we are clear as to what the Holy Spirit is, what the content of the Holy Spirit is, and what the Holy Spirit brings to us when He comes into us. Today God is realized as the Holy Spirit, Christ has become the Holy Spirit, incarnation is in the Holy Spirit, the death of the cross is in the Holy Spirit, resurrection and ascension are in the Holy Spirit, and the Holy Spirit is in us. In other words, in the Holy Spirit are God, man, death, resurrection, and ascension, and because this Holy Spirit is in us, these five things are in us. Every time we live in the Spirit, we live in resurrection. Only when we are in resurrection, in our spirit, can we touch God. The Bible says that God is not the God of the dead but of the living (Matt. 22:32). If we are not in resurrection, we will never be able to touch God. For us to be in resurrection, however, we must be in the Spirit. The Spirit comprises God, man, death, resurrection, and ascension. All these spiritual matters are in the Spirit. In order to touch these spiritual matters, we must touch the Spirit.

In the past we thought that the matter of resurrection was objective and vague and that there was no way for us to touch or comprehend it. But now through the accurate revelation that the Lord has given to His church, we see that resurrection

is in the Holy Spirit and that the Holy Spirit is in us. He is
not merely objective but very subjective. In fact, He is right
inside of us. When we live in resurrection, we live in the Holy
Spirit. In our experience we will feel that resurrection is not
something vague but something real and practical.

THE HOLY SPIRIT DWELLING IN US
BEING DEEPER THAN OUR MIND, EMOTION, AND WILL

God is the Spirit, and today this Spirit is the Spirit of resurrection and the Spirit of ascension. In this Spirit is all that
God is, has, has done, has passed through, and has attained.
This Spirit dwells right inside of us. Romans 8:9 and 11 in the
Chinese Union Version say that the Holy Spirit dwells in our
heart. This is not correct. These two verses in Greek say that
the Holy Spirit dwells in us. In Greek, the Bible rarely says
that the Holy Spirit dwells in our heart (Rom. 5:5; Gal. 4:6).
More often it says that the Holy Spirit dwells in us, that is, in
our spirit.

Romans 8:16 in the Chinese Union Version reads, "The
Holy Spirit Himself witnesses with our heart that we are children of God." Here the correct translation of the word *heart* is
spirit. This proves that the Holy Spirit who lives in us is with
our spirit, because the Holy Spirit witnesses with our spirit.
First Corinthians 6:17 says, "He who is joined to the Lord is
one spirit." Since we have been joined to the Lord as one
spirit, the Lord surely dwells in our spirit.

What is the difference between our spirit and our mind,
emotion, and will? Furthermore, how do we discern between
them? Perhaps when you want to read a book, there may be a
feeling in you telling you not to read it. When you want to go
somewhere, there may be a forbidding in you. When you have
a grudge against a certain brother or sister, there may be
something in you demanding that you be at peace with him or
her. This is our daily experience in our Christian living. Our
mind, emotion, and will are always taking the initiative to
love or to hate, but deep within us we often have a feeling that
is contrary to our mind, emotion, and will. What we like, He
does not agree with, and what we dislike, He demands us
to like. For example, we may dislike a certain brother, but

inwardly we may feel that we should love him, contact him, and fellowship with him. This feeling, which is contrary to our mind, emotion, and will, is the feeling of our spirit. It is the feeling that comes from the Holy Spirit joined to our spirit as one spirit. When our mind, emotion, and will cooperate with and walk according to the feeling of the spirit, our mind, emotion, and will are brought under the ruling and direction of the spirit. As a result, we live in the spirit and in resurrection. This is resurrection.

GOD BEING THE GOD OF THE LIVING

When we live in resurrection in this way, we will sense the presence of God, and we will sense that we have touched God. God is the God of the living, and He can be the God of man and be touched by man only in resurrection. The fact that we can touch God proves that we are in resurrection. Moreover, when we live in resurrection, we will have the clear sense that we are heavenly and that we are in the heavenly realm. We will have a heavenly feeling.

Every time we have an inward feeling—whether it is a forbidding or a charging—and obey it, we will immediately sense resurrection and touch the heavenly sphere. For example, suppose we do not like one brother, but we like another brother. When we see the second brother, we have a beaming smile, but when we see the first brother, we have a frown. Although this is our reaction, inwardly we have the feeling that we should love the first brother and have more fellowship with him and that we should keep a distance from the second brother. If we submit to this feeling, we will immediately sense the presence of God and enjoy the taste of heaven, and we will also sense that we are in the spirit and have touched God and the heavenly sphere. Then in the Lord's table meeting, we will spontaneously render to God our thanks and praises.

However, suppose we sense inwardly that we should have more fellowship with the first brother and reduce our contact with the second brother, but instead we allow our emotions to prefer the second brother and be unhappy when we see the first brother. If we do this, when we come to the Lord's table meeting, we will not be able to open our mouths. Our spirit will not be strong but deflated because we are not living in resurrection. There is no resurrection in us. Rather, there is death, and we are people in death. Therefore, in this kind of situation, God cannot be our God because God is not the God of the dead but of the living.

Every time we live in our spirit, we touch resurrection and the realm of resurrection. When we touch the realm of resurrection, we touch the spiritual realm. Where there is the Holy Spirit, there is resurrection, and where there is the Holy Spirit, there is God and the taste of heaven. God as Spirit comes into our spirit. This Spirit in the New Testament includes everything. All that God is, has, has done, has passed through, and has attained are included in this Spirit. Today this Spirit is in our spirit.

If all the responsible brothers in the different churches would learn to live in the spirit, they would absolutely be in one accord. In most of the churches nine out of ten responsible brothers are not in the one accord. They may have many inward offenses that are not manifested. Why do they lack the one accord? It is because they have not been living in resurrection and in the spirit. It is impossible to have the one accord in the mind, emotion, and will. When the brothers are in the mind, emotion, and will, the best they can do is to refrain from quarreling or talking to one another. Once they speak up, however, they will become furious, which does not help the situation. After a meeting, some brothers may shake their heads and say, "I disagree one hundred percent, but I did not want to say it." This is not the one accord. The genuine one accord is when everyone is in spirit, has learned the lesson, and has been enlightened to see the revelation and vision that the Lord is in resurrection and that He is the God of the living. Resurrection is in the spirit. To live in resurrection is to live in the spirit.

PRACTICALLY EXPERIENCING
DEATH AND RESURRECTION BY SUBJECTING
OUR MIND, EMOTION, AND WILL
TO THE RULING OF THE SPIRIT

We all know that our spirit is deeper than our mind,

emotion, and will and that many times it is contrary to our mind, emotion, and will. To live in the spirit is to go against our mind, emotion, and will, not to enthrone them or give them the preeminence but to have them under the direction of the spirit. If all the responsible brothers in the various churches would practice to live and walk in this way, they would surely have the one accord because the Spirit is only one. If you would live in the spirit, I would live in the spirit, and all of us would live in the spirit, subjecting our mind, emotion, and will to the ruling and direction of the spirit, then we would all be in resurrection and under the ruling of the spirit. Spontaneously, there would be the genuine one accord.

Our mind, emotion, and will comprise everything that is of us—our views, our ideas, our opinions, our thinking, and our likes. Everything that belongs to us, besides God, is included in our mind, emotion, and will. If our mind, emotion, and will are under the ruling of the spirit, we will be in resurrection, and we will touch resurrection. We will truly sense that we have God in us, and we will also sense the presence of heaven. This shows us that resurrection is not objective or abstract. Rather, it is subjective and real because it has entered into our spirit in the Holy Spirit.

If we want to live in our spirit, we must overcome our mind, emotion, and will, go against our mind, emotion, and will, and submit to the ruling of the spirit. When we live in our spirit, we live in resurrection. When we live in resurrection, we enter into God. Then we practically experience death and resurrection. Some saints may have heard the doctrine of our death with Christ, yet they may not live in spirit. They may try to use their own strength to reckon themselves dead, but eventually, the more they reckon themselves to be dead, the more they will live. Hence, they will have no other way but to pray to the Lord and to ask Him to help them and to bind the enemy, to bind the flesh, and to put it to death. Usually, this kind of prayer is never answered, and the Lord never renders such help.

When we learn to live in the spirit, the death of the cross is ours because there is death in resurrection. Where there is resurrection, there is also death. Hence, Paul said, "To know Him and the power of His resurrection and the fellowship of His sufferings, being conformed to His death" (Phil. 3:10). When we live in resurrection, we will experience the Lord's death. We do not need to pay attention to death, because once we enter into resurrection, death becomes our portion.

THE GENUINE CHRISTIAN LIVING BEING A LIVING OF RESURRECTION

Now we have the way. It is up to us whether or not we will walk this way and live this kind of living. We need the Lord's mercy and grace to show us that everything has been accomplished and is in the Holy Spirit and that the Holy Spirit is in us. Today the question is whether we will live by our mind, emotion, and will or, on the contrary, in our spirit. This is the responsibility that we bear.

May the Lord be gracious to us, that by His grace we would live in the spirit, in resurrection, and see that all the spiritual riches are ours. May the Lord grant us all to taste the resurrection power. We have a treasure in us that the excellency of the power may be of God and not out of us (2 Cor. 4:7). The excellency of the power enables us to endure hardship and to bear unbearable afflictions. Whether we face persecution or burdens, this power enables us to be more than conquerors. It is this power that enabled Paul to become a special person. He said that he had seen the Lord of resurrection. He became someone special because the grace of God was with him.

The genuine Christian living is a living of resurrection. A genuine spiritual person is a person in resurrection. One who has authority, power, light, and spiritual reality is one who lives in resurrection, because God, the heavens, the Spirit, and everything are in resurrection. May the Lord open our eyes to see how subjective resurrection is in the Holy Spirit and how practical resurrection is in us. May the Lord grant us the revelation, the vision, and the seeing, and may the Lord bring us into resurrection that all our living and work would be in resurrection.

CHAPTER SIXTEEN

EXPERIENCING DEATH AND ASCENSION IN THE SPIRIT OF RESURRECTION

Scripture Reading: Rom. 6:5, 13; 8:11; Acts 2:33, 36; Eph. 1:20-22.

We have seen that God and everything of God, that is, all that God is, has, has passed through, has accomplished, and has attained, are all stored in the Holy Spirit and have entered into us through the Holy Spirit. Hence, if we want to touch God and everything of God, we must touch the Holy Spirit, because God Himself and all that He has accomplished have been aggregated in the Holy Spirit.

DEATH, RESURRECTION, AND ASCENSION BEING CONNECTED

When we touch the Holy Spirit, we live in resurrection, and only when we are living in resurrection will we have various spiritual experiences. These spiritual experiences are spiritual reality. In other words, we have spiritual reality when we are in resurrection and have spiritual experiences. There are at least five elements in the Holy Spirit—the divine element, the human element, the element of death, the element of resurrection, and the element of ascension. Although death, resurrection, and ascension are three elements, they are connected together as one. Just as we cannot separate death from resurrection, so we cannot separate resurrection from ascension. Most Bible readers know that death is closely connected to resurrection and that resurrection is closely followed by ascension. It is impossible to have resurrection without ascension; ascension and resurrection are connected. Thus, death, resurrection, and ascension are closely connected.

THE DEATH IN ROMANS 6 AND
THE RESURRECTION IN ROMANS 8 BEING CONNECTED

Romans 6 speaks particularly about the death of Christ, but when Christ's death is mentioned, resurrection is also mentioned. Verse 5 says, "For if we have grown together with Him in the likeness of His death, indeed we will also be in the likeness of His resurrection." Once we mention death, we have to mention resurrection, because resurrection and death are connected. This means that all those who experience the death of Christ are those who are raised from the dead. The living of such ones is the living of those who are raised from the dead. Thus, the issue of the death in chapter six is man being brought into resurrection.

Then chapter eight shows us that resurrection is in the Holy Spirit. This chapter particularly speaks of living in the Holy Spirit and shows us that to live in the Holy Spirit is to live in resurrection. Verse 9 says, "If indeed the Spirit of God dwells in you." This Spirit is the Spirit of the One who raised Christ Jesus from the dead, the Spirit of resurrection (v. 11). Hence, when we live in the spirit, we live in resurrection. It is the Spirit of resurrection who raised us up and who not only resurrected our spirit but also brought our whole being into the spirit. In other words, the Spirit of resurrection not only causes every part of our soul to be in the spirit, but one day He will even give life to our mortal bodies.

Therefore we have to see that Romans 8 talks about the Holy Spirit and resurrection and that the Holy Spirit is the Spirit of resurrection. We can see that chapter eight follows chapter six. Chapter six speaks of death, and chapter eight speaks of resurrection. The death in chapter six is connected to the resurrection in chapter eight. Thus, death and resurrection are closely connected to each other. We cannot touch Christ's death without touching Christ's resurrection. If we touch Christ's death, we are in Romans 6, and at the same time, we are also in the resurrection in Romans 8. Death and resurrection are closely connected to each other.

THE RESURRECTION AND ASCENSION
IN ACTS AND EPHESIANS BEING CONNECTED

Resurrection is connected to death, and resurrection is also connected to ascension. We cannot find a place in the entire New Testament that mentions only ascension without mentioning resurrection. Ascension is not a particular topic in the New Testament, but resurrection is, and resurrection is connected to ascension. Resurrection includes ascension. Take the book of Acts for instance. Does this book speak of resurrection or ascension? Did the apostles testify concerning resurrection or ascension? Strictly speaking, Acts is a book on the testimony of the Lord's resurrection. The apostles said that they all were witnesses of the resurrection of Jesus (2:32). Although their testimony was a testimony of resurrection, no other book in the New Testament talks about ascension more clearly than Acts.

In Acts 2 we see how the apostle Peter mentioned the matter of ascension, the whole story of ascension, and the condition of ascension. However, when Peter spoke of ascension, he connected it to resurrection. Ascension is not something independent of resurrection but something dependent on resurrection. Ascension is not its own topic, but resurrection is its own topic, and ascension is a section within the topic of resurrection. Here we clearly see that where there is resurrection, there is ascension and that it is impossible to have resurrection without ascension. In the New Testament resurrection is always connected to ascension.

Ephesians 1 talks about the power of Christ's resurrection (vv. 19-20). This resurrection power raised Christ from the dead and seated Him at God's right hand in the heavenlies, far above all rule and authority and power and lordship and every name that is named, not only in this age but also in that which is to come. This shows us that resurrection brings in ascension and that ascension is connected to resurrection. No one can separate resurrection from ascension.

From this we see that death, resurrection, and ascension are joined together as one. Hence, we can say that there are three main elements in the Holy Spirit—the divine element, the human element, and a "triune" element—the element of death, resurrection, and ascension.

RESURRECTION BEING ACCORDING TO LIFE AND COMING OUT OF LIFE

These three main elements in the Holy Spirit are actually five elements—the divine element, the human element, the element of death, the element of resurrection, and the element of ascension. The Bible mentions many times that the Lord is God, man, and resurrection, but it does not say that the Lord is ascension. Therefore, of the five elements of the Holy Spirit, the Lord occupies three—He is God, man, and resurrection. Moreover, 2 Corinthians 3:17 says, "The Lord is the Spirit." The Lord is God, man, resurrection, and the Spirit. Hence, in the Spirit there are God, man, and resurrection. Before the incarnation God was God, having no human element, but after His incarnation the story of His being God and man began in Bethlehem. At that time He was not only God but also a man. He was a God-man.

When this God-man was on the earth, did He have the element of resurrection in Him? This is a big question in theology. Did the Lord's resurrection life and power exist before His resurrection or after His resurrection? What is the basis of resurrection? Resurrection is according to life and comes from life. For instance, before a flower seed is planted into the soil, there is life within the seed, but does it have the element of resurrection within? Strictly speaking, it does not yet have the element of resurrection within.

Before the Lord's resurrection He had the resurrection life and power within Him, but He had not yet accomplished the matter of resurrection. In John 11:25 He said, "I am the resurrection." This is what the Lord said before His crucifixion and death, but immediately He continued by saying, "[I am] the life." Then in chapter twelve He said that unless the grain of wheat falls into the ground and dies, it abides alone, but if it dies, it bears much fruit (v. 24). Had the Lord been resurrected at that time? The resurrection life was in the "grain of wheat," but the fact of resurrection had not yet been accomplished. It is not until the seed is planted into the ground and grows out from the ground that resurrection is accomplished. This is the expression of life, and the expression of life is resurrection.

From this we see what life and resurrection are. Before the seed is planted into the ground, it has the life of resurrection, but it does not have the resurrection of life. It is only after the seed is planted into the ground and grows out that it has both the life of resurrection and the resurrection of life.

INCARNATION—
GOD BEING MINGLED WITH MAN, AND RESURRECTION—
MAN BEING MINGLED WITH GOD

Before incarnation God had only one element, which was God Himself. After His incarnation He not only had the divine element but also the human element. At that time, because the Lord had not yet died through crucifixion, there was no resurrection. Although He had the resurrection life in Him, the fact of resurrection had not yet been accomplished in Him. After He was raised from the dead, the element of resurrection was added into Him in addition to His divine and human elements. Then there were not only the elements of God and man in Him but also the element of resurrection.

According to God's original intention, He wanted to mingle with man. Hence, He became flesh, obtaining the human element in addition to the divine element. At that point, God had already worked Himself into man, accomplishing the purpose of mingling Himself with man. Why was there a need for the element of resurrection? The reason is that the incarnation of God was only a one-way mingling of God and man. Man had not yet entered into God and been mingled with God. In other words, incarnation put God in the same position as man, but God and man, man and God, had not been fully mingled together. It was only after resurrection that God was fully mingled with man.

When you were saved, your salvation was in the principle of incarnation, which is the bringing of God into man. When you were saved, incarnation took place in you, and God came into you. However, at that moment, was there any mingling between God and you, or you and God? Strictly speaking, according to the principle of incarnation, in our salvation God and man were not mingled together. Instead, God and man were just put together. This may be likened to people baking bread or cakes at home. They first put water into the flour. At this time the water and the flour have merely been put together but not mingled together. After putting the water into the flour, the next step is to mix, blend, and knead them together. At this time the water truly becomes mingled with the flour and the flour with the water. The two—the water and the flour, the flour and the water—are mingled together.

Incarnation brought God into the same position as man. The two were put together but were not fully mingled together. In His thirty-three and a half years of human living, the Lord Jesus was God who had put on man and was living a human life on the earth. God simply came and stayed where man was. Strictly speaking, God and man were not fully mingled together. While the Lord Jesus was living on the earth, His living was the living of the incarnated God. In those thirty-three and a half years, especially in the last three and a half years, the Lord's living, strictly speaking, was not the full living of the mingling of God and man because He had not yet resurrected. At that time God had entered into man, but man had not yet entered into God. This is one side of the matter.

On the other side, the last three and a half years of the Lord's living were truly a living of the mingling of God and man. Thus, there are two aspects. On the one hand, the Lord's living was not the living of the mingling of God and man because the Lord had not yet died and resurrected, and man had not yet entered into God. The incarnation of the Lord brought God into man, but He had not yet died and resurrected and had not yet brought man into God. We can only say that God was living a life in man. Apparently, He first lived on the earth and then died. On the other hand, in reality He died first, and then He lived. At the beginning of His last three and a half years, He was baptized. Baptism put Him to death. When He came up from the water, He was a person of resurrection and was already mingled with God. His living in the last three and a half years on the earth was a living of man being mingled with God.

EXPERIENCING DEATH AND RESURRECTION TO LIVE A LIFE OF THE MINGLING OF GOD AND MAN

Our Christian living is a living in which we first die then live. We died at the time of our baptism. When we believed in the Lord, God entered into us. This is incarnation. From then on, God's goal is to share one living with us, a living of man being mingled with God. Only when man is mingled with God can God be mingled with man. However, if man wants to live a life of being mingled with God, he must die. When we believe in the Lord, the first thing we must do is to be baptized. Romans 6 says that through baptism we died and were raised with the Lord (vv. 3-4). A genuine Christian living is one in which man is mingled with God and in which God mingles with man. Without resurrection, there is no mingling of God and man.

Strictly speaking, incarnation put God and man together but did not fully mingle God and man as one. What kind of procedure can accomplish this matter of mingling God together with man? Only resurrection can. Incarnation simply put God and man in one place but did not fully mingle God and man, man and God, together. It was after resurrection that man entered into God, and God fully mingled with man. God and man were then fully mingled as one. In other words, when we were saved, there was only incarnation in us. There was only Emmanuel—God with man. God and man, man and God, were not yet mingled as one. It was not until the day when man had the element of resurrection that man and God, God and man, were mingled as one. At that time God was not only with man, but God was mingled with man as one.

This shows us that the Holy Spirit's coming into us is for the purpose of mingling God and man together as one. The Holy Spirit possesses both the divine element and the human element, and in addition to the divine and human elements, there is also the element of resurrection. There are the three main elements in the Holy Spirit—the divine element, the human element, and the element of resurrection. When the

Holy Spirit enters into us, He brings God into us, and He also mingles into us the human element, Christ's resurrected humanity. Thus, we may be noble people, because the divine element and the uplifted humanity have been brought into us. Furthermore, there is another element, the element of resurrection. This element includes both death and ascension. Where there is resurrection, there is death, and where there is resurrection, there is ascension. These three elements are one, and their totality is resurrection. All these elements have entered into us through the Holy Spirit that we may be mingled with God in resurrection.

When you contact someone who is living in the Holy Spirit and is filled with the Holy Spirit, you will sense the flavor of God. However, this is not enough. You should also be able to sense the flavor of man in him. All those who are filled with the Holy Spirit know how to be men of the highest standard. A person who is genuinely filled with the Holy Spirit has the flavor of God, the flavor of man, and the flavor of resurrection. He is not snobbish or puffed up but full of love. The more a person is filled with the Holy Spirit, the more he has the human appearance and the human flavor. Not only are the flavors of God and man in him, but the flavor of resurrection is also in him. He is mingled with God. Only in resurrection can man be mingled with God.

THE SIGNS OF BEING IN RESURRECTION— DEATH AND THE HEAVENS

What is the flavor of resurrection? We all know that following resurrection is the heavens and before resurrection is death. There are two kinds of death in the Bible—one comes from Satan whereas the other comes from God. The death that comes from Satan is from Adam and causes us to perish. The death that comes from God is from Christ and causes us to be saved. In other words, the death that comes from Adam causes us to perish, but the death that comes from Christ causes us to receive life. The death in Genesis 2 is a negative death, a perishing death, but the death in Romans 6 is a positive death, a life-receiving death. Many Christians pray unceasingly and even fast and shed tears in order to obtain the death in Romans 6 because they regard such a death as good and precious.

This good and precious death deals with everything in us that is against God, incompatible with God, opposed to God, and of the world, human affections, the self, and the soul-life. When we say that such a death is in a person, we mean that the world, sin, human affections, corruption, and the soul-life have been eliminated and terminated in him. Suppose someone speaks ill of a brother to his face, but that brother does not lose his temper. He remains silent without having to suppress his reaction or exercise patience. This is a sign of death. Such a person lives in resurrection and has the sign of death in him.

Moreover, many times we are able to see the condition of the heavens and savor the taste of the heavens in the saints. Once we see them, we know that they are living in resurrection because we sense the realm of the heavens—a realm that is clear and filled with authority—and we see the mingling of God and man in them. The reality of the mingling of God and man is possible only in the Holy Spirit. However, it is not sufficient to say that this reality is in the Holy Spirit. We must also say that the reality of the mingling is in resurrection. There is no resurrection outside of the Holy Spirit. Resurrection is in the Holy Spirit. The Holy Spirit is resurrection, and resurrection is the Holy Spirit. A person who is filled with the Holy Spirit surely has resurrection in him.

Hence, we can see that a person who is in resurrection surely has two signs—the sign of death and the sign of the heavens. In other words, a person who is in resurrection has the death of the cross as a mark and the condition of the heavens as a sign. Death rids us of anything that is incompatible with God. If we have death, we will not have anything in us that is incompatible with God. The heavens refer to everything in us that is compatible with God. If we have the condition of the heavens, we certainly are those who are compatible with God.

Death is a mark on the negative side, whereas the heavens are a sign on the positive side. Death is the deliverance from the old creation whereas the heavens are the entrance into the new creation. Death delivers us from the old creation, the world, and everything that is of man—which is corrupted, fallen, of human affection, and fleshly. The heavens cause us to enter into the heavenly sphere and to be mingled with God. Therefore, when we see a person who has both death and the heavens in him, we know that he is living in resurrection. To live in the Holy Spirit is to live in resurrection. In the living of such a person, we see the mingling of God and man.

EXPERIENCING DEATH AND ASCENSION IN RESURRECTION

Death is not an independent process but must be experienced in resurrection. Ascension is also not an independent process but must be experienced in resurrection. Some people do not know resurrection, yet all the time they ask for death. Ultimately, they are not able to die, because there is no experience of death apart from resurrection. Only when we are in resurrection can we experience death. The death in Romans 6 can only be experienced in Romans 8. The death in chapter six is merely a fact. By itself, it cannot become our experience in Christ. It is in chapter eight that death becomes our experience in the Holy Spirit and in resurrection. In the same way, we can experience ascension only in resurrection. We cannot pursue the experience of ascension outside of resurrection.

LIVING IN THE SPIRIT

Hence, the experience of death is in resurrection, and the experience of ascension is also in resurrection. Resurrection is the totality of all the Christian experiences. Paul said that he wanted to know the resurrection of Christ (Phil. 3:10), but he did not say that he wanted to know Christ's death or ascension. Rather, he said that he wanted to know the power of His resurrection. If he knew resurrection, he would be conformed to the Lord's death. As long as he knew resurrection, he would be able to experience death and ascension, because death and ascension are in resurrection. Where is resurrection? Resurrection is in the Holy Spirit. Where is the Holy Spirit? The Holy Spirit is in our spirit. Where is our spirit?

Our spirit is in the innermost part of our entire being, deeper even than our soul.

There was once a brother who heard the doctrine of dying and ascending with Christ and was deeply touched. After he went home, he was unable to eat anything, so he knelt down to fast and pray. He cried with sorrow and said, "I have been a Christian for so many years. Why do I not have any experience of death or the heavens?" After he wept, he rose up to read the Bible and looked for all the portions that speak of the heavens and death, and he tried his best to comprehend and understand them. Then he knelt down to pray again, "O Lord, please grant me the taste of death and the taste of the heavens." Do you think this way would work?

This may be likened to listening to lovely music from another person's radio and then going back home to cry and plead for the music again. Will the music come out automatically? Some people said that after the brother in the story above went home to cry and plead, the Spirit came to him. We cannot say that such a thing did not happen, but this is not the proper way that is revealed in the Bible. In another story, a brother testified that from the time he was saved, he became a completely different person in the Holy Spirit. Then another brother admired him, wishing that he could also become a completely different person. So he went to pray and pursue after this. Later he changed himself by talking in a softer voice and doing things in a slower way, seemingly becoming a different person. However, his effort lasted only for three days, and on the fourth day he became exhausted. Eventually, on the fifth day he failed. Some people, after reading spiritual publications and listening to spiritual doctrines, have a desire to practice accordingly and therefore go to pray. However, this is useless. Even the prayer of confession, if it is not in the spirit, may not be profitable, because many times it is the soul that is functioning. We may repent, confess, pursue, and admire merely in our soul. It may be merely the soul that cries, pleads, thinks, and loves. Hence, what matters is not how a certain thing is done but whether we do it in our spirit or in our soul.

We should stop many of our prayers and thoughts because

they may be the activities of our soul. Many people who are used to using their soul have no way to cease from their soul. They are very zealous, they attend every meeting, and they pray long prayers in every meeting, but they cannot touch their spirit. Therefore, those who are zealous should not be too zealous, and those who are not zealous should be more zealous. We must learn not to be carried away in excitement. Rather, we must learn to cease from our emotion, from all the imaginary thoughts in our mind, and from all our high thoughts about ourselves. If we can cease from our soul, this will be a great deliverance. We have to learn to be silent and to turn to our spirit. There we will be able to touch the Holy Spirit and experience all the spiritual reality.

Spiritual experience does not depend on our effort or our running but on our turning to the spirit. This is our unique responsibility. Today God is in our spirit. If we want to contact and touch God, the only way is by turning to our spirit. We do not need to spend an enormous amount of effort to stop our mind, emotion, and will. As long as we turn to our spirit, we will spontaneously touch the Spirit. When we touch the Spirit, that is, when we touch God, we will obey the sense within us. If we always obey the sense, we will live in the spirit and in resurrection. Then the experiences of both death and ascension will be ours, and we will have all the spiritual reality.

CHAPTER SEVENTEEN

THE TWO ASPECTS OF LIFE— WATER AND FIRE

Scripture Reading: Gen. 2:9b-10a; 3:24; Dan. 7:9-10; Luke 12:49-51; John 7:38-39; 1 Cor. 10:4; Rev. 4:5; 22:1-2

Concerning the matter of life, there are two aspects related to our practical need. One is our need for the experience of life, and the other is our need for the revelation of the truth in the Scriptures. If we lack either of these two aspects, it will be difficult for us to have the knowledge of life and the growth in life.

Most Christians who read the Bible confess that the Bible is consistent from beginning to end and has a unique subject. However, although they acknowledge this fact, they often do not agree on what the unique subject and the consistent line are. For this reason, we have to see the central thought of the Bible from the Word of God. The first mention of man in the Bible is concerning man being created in God's image (Gen. 1:26). This implies that the purpose of God in man is to make man exactly the same as He is. At the end of the Bible, at the end of Revelation, we see the completion of God's work in man, in which man is exactly the same as God.

The twenty-two chapters of the book of Revelation can be divided into two main sections. The first three chapters are one section, and the remaining nineteen chapters are another section. The first three chapters speak of Christ being in the church, and chapters four through twenty-two speak of God being in the universe. The first section shows us that Christ is in the midst of the lampstands, and the second section shows us that God is in the universe. At the beginning of the second section, God and the throne of God are mentioned. God

Himself is like a jasper stone (4:3), and there are seven lamps of fire burning before the throne. The seven lamps are the seven Spirits of God (v. 5). This picture depicts the work of God in the universe. This work comes from the One who is like a jasper stone in appearance and from the throne where the fire comes forth. This work begins from chapter four and continues through chapter twenty-one and produces a city that surrounds the throne. The wall of the city is also made of jasper (21:18), having the same color as God in appearance.

GOD'S PURPOSE IN THE UNIVERSE

The purpose of God in the universe is to produce a group of people who will be exactly the same as He is. In terms of image, they will be the same as He is. He is jasper, and they will also be jasper. In terms of radiance and color, they will also be the same as He is. Whatever kind of glory He has, they will also have. In other words, the condition of these people will be the same as that of God.

In Revelation 4 the One who is sitting on the throne, having the appearance of a jasper stone, is the same as the jasper wall of the city in chapter twenty-one. At the beginning of the universe God was sitting on the throne, and only He had the appearance of a jasper stone, but at the end of God's work in the universe, a jasper wall is produced. The jasper wall surrounds the One on the throne who is like a jasper stone, indicating that God will eventually gain or produce a group of people who are exactly the same as He is. Once this issue comes forth, the new heavens and new earth will come, and the eternal rest will begin, because God will have accomplished and fulfilled His eternal purpose. This is the unique subject of the Bible.

THE UNIQUE SUBJECT OF THE BIBLE—
MAKING MAN THE SAME AS GOD

In Romans

The unique purpose of God in the universe is to make man exactly the same as He is. This is the unique subject of the Bible. According to this unique subject, the Bible has a consistent line, which is the line of life. The Bible speaks of this matter from beginning to end. For example, Romans 8:30 says, "Those whom He predestinated, these He also called; and those whom He called, these He also justified; and those whom He justified, these He also glorified." Those whom God predestinated were called by God at a certain time. Why did God predestinate them? God predestinated them that they would be conformed to the image of the Son of God (v. 29). God chose us, predestinated us, and called us for the purpose that we would be conformed to the image of His Son. God wants us to be conformed to the image of His Son. His Son is the mold of the image. No one has ever seen God, but the Son of God has declared Him (John 1:18). Colossians 1:15 says that the Son of His love is "the image of the invisible God." The Son of God is the image of God, and the image of God is the Son of God. Hence, God wants to make us exactly the same as His Son.

In Corinthians

Second Corinthians 3:18 says, "But we all with unveiled face, beholding and reflecting like a mirror the glory of the Lord, are being transformed into the same image from glory to glory, even as from the Lord Spirit." After we are saved, the Holy Spirit works in us that we may be transformed into the image of the Lord. This transformation is of the Lord's Spirit and is the work of the Holy Spirit in us. The Holy Spirit will continuously work in us until we are completely transformed and even our body is redeemed and conformed to the Lord's body of glory. First John 3:2 says, "If He is manifested, we will be like Him." Hence, at the end of Revelation, we see that all God's redeemed people are like jasper stone, being exactly the same as the image of God. This is the unique subject in the Bible. From beginning to end God works in us to fulfill this unique purpose—to make every one of us the same as He is.

THAT MAN MAY BE THE SAME AS GOD
IN LIFE, NATURE, APPEARANCE, AND RADIANCE

When the Bible mentions that the Lord Jesus is the Son of God, there are two points of significance. First, He is the image of God. Colossians 1:15 says that the Lord Jesus is the image of the invisible God, and Hebrews 1:3 tells us that He is the impress of God's substance. The second point of significance is that the life of God is in Jesus, His Son.

The image and the life of God are in His Son; thus, God, who wants us to also be His sons, requires the same of us. On the one hand, He works in us that we may have His image, and on the other hand, He causes us to have His life. Only those who have God's life and image can be exactly the same as He is. This is the reason that God gave us His eternal life. The purpose is that we may be like Him. In other words, the unique purpose of God's being in us is to work in us to the extent that we would be the same as He is in life, nature, image, and radiance.

Perhaps some people are not able to take this word, thinking that, regardless of how much we have been saved, man is still man, and God is still God, and man cannot be saved to the degree that he will be the same as God. However, Revelation clearly unveils this matter to us. The One sitting on the throne is like a jasper stone, and the wall of the city is also jasper stone. Both the wall of the city and the One who is sitting on the throne are like jasper stone. This means that we saved ones will one day be exactly the same as God. Not only will we see God's glory, but God's glory will become our glory, and we will be the same as God in life, nature, appearance, radiance, and even outward expression.

The beginning of Revelation mentions the "jasper God," and the end mentions the "jasper city." The jasper God becomes the center of the jasper city, and the jasper city becomes the perimeter of the jasper God. The jasper God is in the center, the jasper city is the perimeter, and the glory of God shines forth through the city. God and the city are completely one. The appearance, radiance, and nature of the city are absolutely the same as that of God. God and man are mingled together. God is in man, and man is in God. God is the content of man, and man is the expression of God. God is the center, and man is the perimeter.

Many of the visions and stories in the Bible are related to this. When we touch this matter, the whole Bible is linked together, and all the spiritual experiences are also linked together. The incarnation of the Lord Jesus was for this. His death on the cross and the shedding of His blood to bear man's sin were for this. His resurrection, ascension, and becoming the life-giving Spirit were for this. He is saving sinners, edifying the saints, giving us grace, gifts, life, power, light, and vision for this. This matter is the center of the entire Bible. All the truths of the Bible hang securely on this because this matter is the center of God. The unique purpose of God in the universe is to make man the same as He is. This is the unique subject of the Bible.

THE CONSISTENT LINE IN THE BIBLE BEING LIFE

The consistent line in the Bible is life. Apart from life, there is no other way for God to accomplish this goal of making man the same as He is. Only through the way of life can God's life be wrought into man to operate, transform, and cause a metabolic reaction in man, so that man may be transformed and become the same as God.

In Genesis 1 when man is mentioned, the image of God is also mentioned (v. 26). Then in chapter two when man is mentioned again, immediately life is mentioned (v. 7). Only when God's life enters into man can man have the genuine image of God. Only when God's life enters into man can man be the same as God in nature, appearance, radiance, and color. Thus, Genesis 1 and 2 mention the image of God on the one hand and the life of God on the other. In chapter two after God created man, He put man in front of the tree of life. This indicates that God wanted man to be the same as He by means of this life. For man to be the same as God in nature, appearance, radiance, and color, he must allow God's life to enter into him.

The city of the New Jerusalem in Revelation 21 is composed of jasper and precious stones, signifying that we redeemed ones are jasper and precious stones. In Genesis 2, however, the Adam who was created by God and who was in the garden of Eden was a man of clay, a muddy man. Many people, after being saved, admire the condition of Adam in the garden of Eden, but they do not realize that the Adam who was in the garden of Eden did not have the life of God. In other words, he was merely clay, not gold or precious stone.

There is no comparison between us, who are also men of clay, and Adam who was in the garden of Eden, because even though he was a man of clay, he was not ruined or filthy like us. If we made a doll out of clay, at first it would be pretty and complete. But then if some children hug it, kiss it, and touch it with their hands, it will very quickly lose its shape. Its nose may drop off, and its ears may fall down. The "clay doll" in the garden of Eden was a complete doll, but we "clay dolls" who are outside of the garden of Eden were born filthy and crippled. Thus, we cannot be compared with Adam. However, we now have the gold, pearl, and precious stone in us. Although the "clay Adam" in the garden of Eden was good, the gold, bdellium (which corresponds to the pearl), and precious stones were outside of him and were not in him.

THE WATER OF LIFE AND THE FIRE OF LIFE

God put Adam in front of the tree of life because He wanted Adam to eat of the tree of life and receive it into him. Once the tree of life enters into man, it becomes a river of living water that waters and transforms man and eventually brings forth the gold, pearl and precious stones. This is the story in Genesis 2. Although the gold and precious stones were the issue of the flow of life, they did not flow into Adam. Because God's life had not entered into Adam, the gold, pearl, and precious stones were outside of Adam.

Then in chapter three the evil one came and caused Adam to contact the tree of the knowledge of good and evil. Before the tree of life could enter into Adam, the tree of the knowledge of good and evil came into him. In this way, the river of water of life disappeared, and what emerged was the sword of fire (3:24). Originally, in front of the tree of life was a river of living water (2:10), but due to Adam's fall, something of Satan entered into man, and the river of water of life became a flame.

Revelation 4 mentions the throne of God and the seven lamps of fire before the throne. Then chapter twenty-two mentions the throne of God again, saying that there is a river of water of life proceeding out of the throne of God. There are two main sections in Revelation. At the beginning, Revelation says that there is fire coming from the throne of God, and at the end, it says that there is water proceeding out of the throne of God (22:1). In Daniel 7 the vision that Daniel saw was the same as what John saw at the beginning of Revelation—a stream of fire issuing forth and coming out from the throne of God (vv. 9-10). However, at the end of Revelation, what comes forth from the throne is not fire but water.

After God created Adam, He put him before the tree of life. From the tree of life flowed a river that had four branches flowing in four directions—east, west, north, and south. The flowing of these four branches produced gold, pearl, and precious stones. The description of the New Jerusalem at the end of Revelation also mentions the tree of life and the river of water of life flowing through the four corners of the holy city. Furthermore, the materials of the city are pure gold, pearl, and precious stones, which are the same materials in the river in Genesis. In Genesis 2 the gold, pearl, and precious stones had not yet entered into Adam, the man of clay, but in Revelation 21 the man of clay is no longer there but has been completely transformed into pure gold, pearl, and precious stones.

In Genesis 2, if man had come to the tree of life, he would have touched the river. But in chapter three, after man's fall, if man wanted to contact the tree of life, he would have touched the flaming sword that turned in every direction (v. 24). What is the flaming sword? The flaming sword does one thing—a killing work. It is both a flame and a sword, a sword and a flame. Its nature is a flame, and its function is to kill. In other words, if man had touched the tree of life in Genesis 2, he surely would have touched the river of life. But if man wanted to touch the tree of life in chapter three, he would have touched the flame that burns and kills man. Thus, there was a flaming sword. Ever since that time, this river sometimes appears as a flame and sometimes as water. Its condition varies greatly. Hence, from the throne of God proceeds a river that is sometimes the water of life that gives life and sometimes a flame that burns and kills.

In John 7 the Lord came in order to give man the living water. He said, "If anyone thirsts, let him come to Me and drink. He who believes into Me, as the Scripture said, out of his innermost being shall flow rivers of living water" (vv. 37b-38). The Lord has given His life to man as living water. In chapter four the Lord also answered the Samaritan woman with the eternal life. He said, "Whoever drinks of the water that I will give him shall by no means thirst forever; but the water that I will give him will become in him a fountain of water gushing up into eternal life" (v. 14). What the Lord meant was that the eternal life is the living water.

However, in Luke 12 the Lord said, "I have come to cast fire on the earth, and how I wish that it were already kindled!" (v. 49). Then He continued, saying, "Do you think that I have come to give peace on the earth? No, I tell you, but rather division" (v. 51). This means that the Lord as fire burns in man to give rise to division. Sometimes the husband opposes the wife, or the wife opposes the husband. Sometimes the parents oppose the children, or the children oppose the parents. When this fire is cast into man, it burns in man and gives rise to conflicts among the believing and unbelieving relatives. This is the Lord's life. The condition of some Christians, however, is like a bag filled with water—they can neither be kindled nor burned because they know the Lord's life only as water but not as fire. Those who do know the Lord's life as fire that has been kindled and is burning within them often have emotional conflicts with their unbelieving relatives. Therefore, the fire in Luke 12 is the Lord's life. John said that the Lord's life is water, and Luke said that the Lord's life is fire. Are these two lives? No, they are one life, but sometimes this life is water and other times it is fire.

THE SPIRIT OF LIFE

This life is water, this life is fire, and this life is also the Holy Spirit. God is Spirit, and when He is touched by man, He is life. John 7 tells us that the river of living water is the Holy Spirit (vv. 38-39). On the day of Pentecost, the Holy Spirit was poured out. The Bible speaks of the Holy Spirit being "poured out" upon all flesh (Acts 2:17). This indicates that the Holy

Spirit is like pouring rain. However, on the day that the Holy Spirit was poured out in the house where the disciples were gathered, what the disciples saw was not water but fire. "And there appeared to them tongues as of fire, which were distributed; and it sat on each one of them; and they were all filled with the Holy Spirit" (vv. 3-4). The fire is the living water.

Revelation 4:5 mentions that there are seven lamps of fire before the throne and that the seven lamps are the seven Spirits of God. Seven denotes that the function is complete. We all know that the Spirit of God is not seven but one. The fire in the seven lamps of fire is also not seven but one. The seven lamps of fire come out from the throne. Chapter four verse 5 clearly says that the seven lamps of fire are the seven Spirits of God. The fire is the Spirit, and this fire is the seven Spirits. Both chapters four and five say that this fire is the Spirit of God. Then chapter twenty-two again speaks of the throne and the river of water of life, bright as crystal, which proceeds out of the throne. Are there two rivers coming out of the throne, or is there only one river? According to the consistent line of the Scriptures, there should not be two rivers but one. This river is sometimes fire and sometimes water. The water and the fire are one. They are the Spirit of God.

Chapters four and five mention the One who is sitting on the throne, the Lamb, and the seven eyes. The seven eyes are the seven Spirits of God. Then at the beginning of chapters twenty-one and twenty-two, God and the Lamb are mentioned but not the Spirit. Where is the Spirit? The Spirit is the river that proceeds out of the throne of God. Hence, what flows into us is the Spirit. When the Spirit enters into us, He is life. God has flowed out. When He flows to man, He is the Spirit, and when He flows into man and is received and touched by man, He is life.

LIFE BEING FIRE WHERE SATAN IS
AND BEING WATER WHERE SATAN IS NOT

When this river, which is the Spirit of God or the life of God, flows out, it is sometimes water and sometimes fire. When is it water, and when is it fire? In the first two chapters of Genesis, before Satan came into the scene, this river was a river of water. Then at the end of Revelation, in chapters twenty-one and twenty-two, after Satan is terminated, this river is also a river of water. Then when does this flow become fire? Apparently, wherever Satan is, this flow of life is fire, and wherever Satan is not, this flow of life is water. Where Satan is, this life is fire, and where Satan is not, this life is water.

Before Genesis 3 this flow was water, and in Revelation 21 and 22, this flow is also water. From Genesis 3 to Revelation 20 this flow is both fire and water. Fire was mentioned in Genesis 3 for the first time. After Revelation 21:8 there is no further mention of fire because Satan, death, and Hades have already been cast into the lake of fire.

THE TWO ASPECTS OF LIFE— THE WATERING OF THE WATER AND THE BURNING OF THE FIRE

Water refers to God's life watering us and transforming us inwardly, and fire refers to God's life burning, purging, and eliminating everything of Satan in us. These are the two aspects of the function of God's life in us. On the one hand, the water of life enters into us and flows God's nature and content into us. This water supplies us and waters us, flowing God's riches and content into us. The gold, pearl, and precious stones in Genesis 2 are the issue of the flow of life. Wherever the water flows, there is gold, pearl, and precious stones. These are the contents of God's life.

It is through the flow of the water of life that the content, color, radiance, appearance, and nature of God's life can enter into man. When this life flows into us, it flows God's content into us to supply us. The more God's life passes through us and the stronger the flow, the more gold, pearl, and precious stones there are, and the more God's nature, color, radiance, and appearance increase in us. This is the watering, supplying, and transforming aspect of the flowing of life in us.

On the other hand, when this flow of life enters into us, it has another function—the function of fire. Hence, this flow is also fire. What is the function of fire? Fire burns, consumes, and eliminates things. Why is there a need for burning? It is because Satan has come in. Due to man's fall, Satan brought in the world, sin, the flesh, and many things that belong to him and that oppose God. Consequently, man has become impure and complicated. He is full of Satan, the world, sin, and the flesh. On the one hand, God's life flows His nature, appearance, radiance, and color into us to supply us and transform us from men of clay to men of gold. On the other hand, because the world, sin, the flesh, and everything of Satan have entered into us, when the life flows into us, it is like fire burning in us.

Why does Luke 12 say that when the Lord's fire is kindled in us, we will experience emotional conflict with our relatives? This happens because in many cases, they love the world, but we do not, and they love the pleasures of sin, but we do not. As a result, our relatives may rise up to oppose us, creating a conflict with us. The fire burns away the world, sin, and the flesh in us, which are of Satan, and eventually, there is dissension, disharmony, and discord between us and our relatives. Our relatives will have a negative feeling toward us because we do not love the world or enjoy the pleasures of sin with them. In this way we will lose the peace with them.

On the day of Pentecost the Holy Spirit was poured out like a hard rain, but the disciples described it as fire. When Peter and the eleven apostles spoke to the men of Judea and those who were dwelling in Jerusalem, those who listened were pricked in their heart and confessed their sins. Thus, the Holy Spirit comes for the burning of man's sins.

EXPERIENCING THE WATERING OF THE WATER OF LIFE AND THE BURNING OF THE FIRE OF LIFE

The Spirit is one, and this life also is one, but in the matter of supplying, this life is sometimes like water and sometimes like fire. When this life waters and supplies us inwardly, it enables us to touch the presence of God and transforms us so that our mind, emotion, and will are like God's. At the same time, this life also burns in us, burning away our flesh, self, and corruption.

In our actual experience, many times we feel that this life in us is like water that quenches our thirst. When we are thirsty, He is there watering us, and when we are weak, He is there empowering us. In this way we experience the presence of God so that what we think, what we love, what we incline to, and what we desire match the condition of God. Then our inner being is comfortable, satisfied, living, fresh, bright, strong, and powerful. This is the issue of the supply of the water of life and the condition of our being filled with the water.

Sometimes, however, the Spirit as the fire burns in us, making us sorrowful and uncomfortable so that we grieve and abhor ourselves on the one hand and desperately want to do something for the Lord on the other. More than twenty years ago, for several months I went to pray on a hill every morning. At that time the fire was especially burning within me, and I would pray and weep at the same time. On the one hand, I was willing to live for the Lord and preach the gospel for the Lord, but on the other hand, I abhorred myself, feeling that I was so corrupted and that every bad thing or matter in the world was in me. This was the taste of the fire burning in me. In this way I had a genuine repentance and confession.

If we confess merely because we have heard the doctrine about confession, our confession is something taught, something that is the result of persuasion. It is not the issue of the burning of the Holy Spirit in us. When the Holy Spirit burns in us, we do not need people to tell us that we are sinful. Instead, we will confess that we are sinful, filthy, and evil and that our sins far exceed the sins of others. This kind of humble confession is real only in Spirit. Not only so, this fire also burns away our flesh and our disposition.

Before Satan came into man, it was sufficient for this life to be merely water. At that time man had not been mutated and did not have the evil element in him. Second Corinthians 4:7 says, "We have this treasure in earthen vessels." *Earthen vessels* denotes vessels made of clay, which indicates that we are made of clay. In the garden of Eden before he sinned, Adam was also a vessel of clay, an earthen vessel. But after Satan entered into Adam, this vessel of clay became a corrupted vessel.

In Genesis 4 we see the murder of Abel, showing that

something of Satan had come in (v. 8). Hence, from Genesis 3 to Revelation 20, Satan walks with man and follows man. Man and Satan are linked together. When God's life comes into man, this life is water to God and fire to Satan. Water brings in the supply of God's life, and fire burns away everything of Satan. Thus, after Satan entered into man in Genesis 3, the flow of fire came in. Then after Satan is cast out from man in Revelation 20, the flow of fire disappears. Instead, a river of water of life proceeds out of the throne of God. What flows out is the Spirit, and what flows into us is life. This life in us is sometimes like water and sometimes like fire. When our inner being is pure, and we reject evil and do not mind the flesh, the water flows through us to water and supply us in order that we would be fresh, bright, strong, at peace, and satisfied. However, when the things of Satan—the world, sins, and the flesh—hang on us, the life in us is like fire burning in us. This is our experience.

Today we have not yet arrived at Revelation 21; we have still not come to chapter twenty. We still have sins, the flesh, the world, and many things of Satan in us. Hence, this life is always burning in us as fire. After the burning, the water comes. Our experience is always like this—the more burning there is, the more our inner being is living, fresh, and bright, and the more peace, satisfaction, and comfort we have.

Hence, after the burning of the fire, the water comes. The water and the fire are not two rivers but one. One day there will no longer be fire. Everything of Satan will be terminated in us. This will be our transfiguration, in which we will be delivered from our flesh and the old creation. When everything of Satan is put off in us, there will no longer be fire; instead there will be water proceeding out of the throne of God and of the Lamb. When this water flows out, it is the Spirit, and when it flows into us, it is life.

Today eternity has not yet arrived, but we can have a foretaste of the eternal power. May the Lord have mercy on us that while we are still living on the earth, we would be living in spiritual reality and in a spiritual condition, being able to see one thing—whether it be fire or water—coming out of God and passing through the Lamb. That which comes from

God and the Lamb is the Spirit, and the Spirit enters into us as life, the life of God. This life is sometimes like fire that burns us and sometimes like water that waters us. When we are pure inwardly, He is the water of supply, but when there is mixture in us, He is the burning fire. May we all see these two aspects of life—the watering of the water and the burning of the fire.

CHAPTER EIGHTEEN

REVELATION AND EXPERIENCE

Scripture Reading: Eph. 1:17-23; 3:16-19

We can see the matter of prayer throughout the entire New Testament. We see the Lord's prayer in the Gospels, which focuses on the principles of prayer. We also see the Lord's prayer in Gethsemane and the two prayers of the apostle Paul in Ephesians. Among all these prayers, the two prayers in Ephesians can be said to be the most practical and complete prayers in the New Testament.

THE TWO PRAYERS IN EPHESIANS

There are two prayers in Ephesians—one in chapter one and the other in chapter three. The prayer in chapter one focuses on revelation, and the prayer in chapter three focuses on experience. In the prayer in chapter one, the apostle asks God for spiritual revelation that we may see that God has to work in us to the extent that we become the inheritance of His glory. In the prayer in chapter three, the apostle asks God to strengthen us through His Spirit into our inner man that we may experience the power in us which has already been manifested. This power is all that God has accomplished in Christ. There is no other passage like Ephesians 1 that is able to tell us in such a precise and complete way what God has accomplished in Christ.

The Prayer for Revelation in Chapter One

Ephesians 1:19-23 says, "And what is the surpassing greatness of His power toward us who believe, according to the operation of the might of His strength, which He caused to operate in Christ in raising Him from the dead and seating

Him at His right hand in the heavenlies, far above all rule
and authority and power and lordship and every name that is
named not only in this age but also in that which is to come;
and He subjected all things under His feet and gave Him to
be Head over all things to the church, which is His Body, the
fullness of the One who fills all in all." There is a power in
Christ which caused Him to be raised, to ascend, to be far
above all things, and to be Head over all things, and which
also caused the church to become His mystical Body, the fullness of the One who fills all in all. Today this accomplishing
power is also toward us who believe. However, we may not be
able to see all the matters that God in Christ is working out
in us. For this, the apostle prayed to God that we would have
revelation.

The Prayer for Experience in Chapter Three

Then in chapter three the apostle prayed that God, according to this revelation, would grant us the experience, because
it is one thing for God to work something out in us, but it is
another thing for us to experience it personally. God gives us
the revelation and seeing in order that we may have the experience. Many of us, however, not only do not have the
experience but also do not have the seeing. Regarding the two
prayers in Ephesians, we may be absolutely inexperienced.
There are many Christians who are able to recite the Lord's
prayer but who do not have any understanding of the apostle's
prayers. They often recite the Lord's prayer, but they do not
care for these two prayers which are of the highest spiritual
standard. Today we who are in the Lord's recovery must know
these two prayers.

The Two Prayers Focusing
on the Mingling of God and Man

These two prayers are centered on the same matter, which
is God in Christ working Himself into us. The emphasis of the
first prayer is on revelation and seeing, and the emphasis of
the second prayer is on experience and enjoyment. This is
what we must see clearly. These two prayers touch the same
matter, which is the mysterious God in Christ working out an

exceedingly great mystery in us. This matter first requires our seeing and then our experience.

For us to have the seeing and the experience, the apostle uttered two special prayers—one in chapter one, which is a prayer for revelation, and the other in chapter three, which is a prayer for experience. These two prayers touch only one thing. The most obvious point of similarity is that the issue mentioned at the end of both prayers is the filling. The first prayer ends with the church being the fullness of the One who fills all in all, and the second prayer ends with us being filled unto all the fullness of God. From this we see that even though the wording of these two prayers is different, their result—that God in Christ is filling us—is absolutely consistent. God and we, we and God, will be completely mingled together, and we will be filled unto all the fullness of God. The ultimate result of these two prayers touches this same matter.

As for us, first we need the seeing, which is why the apostle prayed for us regarding revelation, and second, we need the experience, which is why the apostle prayed for us regarding experience. Both prayers touch the great mystery of God mingling with man. The first one is regarding revelation for our seeing, and the second is regarding experience for our enjoyment.

Asking for a Spirit of Wisdom and Revelation

The first prayer is for a spirit of wisdom and revelation (1:17-18). Revelation is for seeing, and wisdom is for understanding. For example, suppose there is a radio sealed in a box so that we are not able to see it. Since we cannot see the radio, we have no revelation concerning it. If we open the box and put the radio in front of us, we will be able to see it. This is to have revelation. However, for us to understand what is inside of the radio, we still need wisdom. A person who has studied electricity would be able to understand the radio by looking at it, but someone unlearned in electricity would be unable to understand it no matter how much he looked at it. Even though he may see it, he would not understand it. This is to have revelation but no wisdom. A person who has studied electricity has the wisdom before he has the revelation because his mind has been trained to have the knowledge of electricity. We can say that he has the wisdom of electricity in his mind. When the radio is "revealed" to him, he is able to understand it immediately. This is to first have the wisdom and then the revelation. After he sees the radio, he is able to understand it.

The mystery that God is working out in us in Christ is so great and wonderful that it requires not only our seeing but also our understanding. Hence, we need revelation, and we also need wisdom. Regarding many spiritual matters, we often hear of them but lack the inward understanding. The reason is that we are short of spiritual wisdom, and our mind is not exercised enough and is not experienced in spiritual matters. Thus, even though we may have heard these things again and again, inwardly we still may not understand.

When some people first learn how to sing, they think that every musical note is the same. Their ears can hardly tell the differences in pitch because their ears are not experienced. Some people's ears are experienced in listening to gossip but not to music, because their ears have been exercised for several decades to listen to gossip but not to music. When you talk about business trade with some brothers, they can fully understand you, even if you mention only a few words. They are able to say things in a more precise, concise, and thorough way because their minds are experienced in business. When some saints get angry and scold people, their voices are loud, forceful, and full of confidence because they are experienced in this matter. But if we asked them to speak for God and to speak the grace of God, they would be speechless. Even though they may say something, they would not say it clearly and to the point. This shows us that we are most experienced in the matters in which we exercise our mind and our understanding. For this reason, our mind has to be exercised in the spiritual matters.

GOD'S POWER TOWARD US

In the prayer of Ephesians 1 Paul mentioned three great points. When these three great points are put together, we can see that the burden is that we would truly know God. First, we have to know His calling. Second, we have to know that He wants to gain us as His inheritance. Third, we have to know His power toward us (vv. 18-19). The power of God toward us is the power of God toward Christ. In other words, the kind of power that God had toward Christ is the kind of power God has toward us. This means that today the work that God is doing in us is nothing less than the work that God did in Christ. The power of God toward Christ in the past was exactly the same as the power of God toward us today. What God did in Christ in the past is what He is doing in us today. What God is doing in us is what He did in Christ. The power of God toward Christ is now also toward us.

The power of God toward Christ accomplished several major events in Christ. First, it raised Christ from the dead. Second, it seated Him at God's right hand in the heavenlies. Third, it caused Him to be far above all rule and authority and power and lordship and every name that is named not only in this age but also in that which is to come. Fourth, it subjected all things under His feet. Fifth, it gave Him to be Head over all things to the church. Sixth, it caused the church to be His Body, the fullness of the One who fills all in all (vv. 20-23).

The power of God that operates in us is the power that He caused to operate in Christ. This power caused Christ to be raised, to ascend, to be far above all things, and to be Head over all things to the church. It also caused the church to be His Body. Now the power that God caused to operate in Christ is also being applied to us. This power still has the same effect on us today. Hallelujah! The power that caused Christ to be raised from the dead, to ascend to the heavens, to be far above all, and to be Head to the church is also toward us. This power is so great!

THE CHURCH AS THE BODY OF CHRIST BEING PRODUCED FROM RESURRECTION

Since the church is the Body of Christ and our service is the service of the church, we have the realization that the service of the church is the service of the Body, the service in coordination. When we come to the meeting hall, you may sweep the floor, I may arrange the chairs, and another brother may clean the door. This kind of coordination is the service of the Body, the service of the church. One time at the meeting hall we saw that many saints were busy cleaning and tidying up the meeting hall. One brother marveled and said, "Look, what a beautiful scene! Some are sweeping the floor, some are arranging the chairs, and some are cleaning the windows." This is an example of the service of the Body of Christ being realized by us.

What is the Body of Christ? Before His resurrection, Christ did not have a Body. He was an individual. It was after His resurrection, ascension, transcending over all things, and becoming the Head of all things and of the church that He gained a mystical Body. The church as the mystical Body of Christ is the fullness of the One who resurrected, ascended, transcended over all things, who is above all things, and who fills all in all. The Body, the church, the mystical Body of Christ, is something that has been resurrected, has ascended, and is now transcendent over all things and above all things. The church was produced after the resurrection of Christ. From Ephesians we know that the church is something very high and that the procedure through which the church was produced is marvelous. The producing of the church was not that simple.

In short, the church, the Body of Christ, was produced after Christ resurrected, ascended, transcended over all things, and was made Head over all things. Christ's resurrection, ascension, transcending over all things, and being Head over all things are all for the church. What is the church? The church is His Body. It was in Christ's resurrection and ascension that He became the Head of the church, and it was at this time that Christ, the Head of all things, obtained a Body. This Body is the church.

From this we see that the church was not produced from a low situation. Christ was incarnated and born in a manger, but it was not possible for the church to be produced in this way. Christ in His incarnation was born in the lowest position, but the church was not produced in the same way. The birth of the church was very high. The church was produced in the highest realm—in the realm of His resurrection, His ascension, His transcending over all things, and His being Head over all things. The status of the church is very high, and the position of the church is very noble. In other words, the church was produced in resurrection, and it was produced starting from resurrection and ending with His transcending over all things and being Head over all things. It was at that time that the Body, the church, was produced.

Without resurrection, there would be no church. The church came out of resurrection and must also pass through resurrection. This is what Ephesians 1 says. If we do not see that resurrection was the realm in which the church was produced, we cannot understand the prayer in Ephesians 1. At the end of the prayer there is something mystical—the fullness of the One who fills all in all, which is the church. The church did not exist before resurrection. Before resurrection there was only Christ, and His body was finite, not mystical. It was after Christ's resurrection, ascension, transcending over all things, and becoming the Head over all things that a mystery emerged. This mystery is the Body of Christ, which is the church.

The church, the Body of Christ, is of resurrection. The church began with Christ's resurrection, proceeded with His ascension to the heavenlies to be far above all things and to be the Head over all things, and was eventually brought forth. Hence, the church began with resurrection and was produced from resurrection.

THE CHURCH AND THE SERVICE OF THE CHURCH DEPENDING ON OUR LIVING IN THE SPIRIT

Resurrection produces the church. Resurrection is in the Holy Spirit, and the Holy Spirit is in us. Suppose we all came together to serve in coordination. Some would sweep the floor, some would clean the windows, and some would visit people. All different kinds of service and work would be expressed here. We might say that this is the Body of Christ and the service of the church, but is it correct to say this? If all these activities and services are done in the Spirit, then they are the service of the church, but if they are not done in the Spirit, then they are not the service of the church. This is because it is only in the Spirit that we can touch resurrection, and it is only in resurrection that there can be the church.

Although we have been saved, have Christ's life, and are Christians, for us to live the church life and to have the service of the church, we must live in the Spirit. When we live in the Spirit, we live in resurrection, and only when we live in resurrection can we have the service of the church. For example, when we go to a certain locality and see that the saints there are all zealous, diligent, and capable, that some are busy doing this and some doing that, and that everyone is harmonious in their coordination, we may praise them and say, "This church is very good. Their service truly expresses the Body of Christ." If we draw the conclusion that this is the service of the church merely because of the outward condition, we are still inexperienced.

For example, suppose you take a piece of yellow metal to a jewelry shop. Would the shop owner immediately nod and acknowledge that it is gold? Of course he would not. He would examine it first. Today, however, the situation is not like this. It seems that when many people see something yellow, they say that it is gold without paying attention to whether it is bronze or gold, hollow or solid. As long as it is yellow, they say that it is gold. This is the poor condition we are in. When we see people doing things in the meeting hall and the saints busily working, we immediately praise them and say, "This church is very good. This is the service of the Body, the service in coordination, and the corporate service." Actually, this is the speaking of an inexperienced person. We know that in order to ascertain whether something is gold, it is not sufficient to merely observe the outward color. We need to see its inner essence. Hence, we not only need to pay attention to the zealous coordination and diligent service of the saints, but we also have to see whether or not they do these things in the spirit. If they do these things in the spirit, then in that place there will be the church and the service of the church. But if they do these things outside of the spirit, then in that place there will not be the church or the service of the church.

For example, the saints in a certain locality may be very sincere and diligent in service and coordination, but they may do these things in their natural energy and according to their preference. They may be natural and not in their spirit. If this is the case, they may maintain their sincerity, diligence, and coordination for three weeks, but afterward, they will not be able to coordinate with one another. Experience tells us that this kind of situation happens all the time. One time we saw a group of saints coordinating in harmony, loving one another, and being affectionate toward one another, even to the degree that they seemed to be "glued" to one another and inseparable. Although this was the outward situation, we worried that they would eventually break up. As expected, they started to fight with one another in less than a month. This one accused that one, and that one accused this one, and they bit and devoured one another. What does this prove? This proves that their initial coordination was in the flesh, in the natural man, in their preference, and in their emotion, not in the spirit.

Suppose someone comes to serve and cleans the meeting hall. Then after you compliment him, he comes again the next day before suppertime. After you praise him some more, he comes again before two o'clock on the third day, and he feels happy and sweet. Unfortunately, a few days later, due to something improper in his service, he receives some adjusting that touches his inward feeling. Then he becomes discouraged and disheartened. Not only does he come very late on the next day, but he disappears on the third day, and eventually he does not come anymore. This indicates that his serving in zeal was not in the spirit but outside of the spirit.

The genuine one accord does not come from gritting one's teeth or closing one's eyes. Some Christians maintain the oneness of the church by gritting their teeth or even closing their eyes, because once they open their eyes, they are not able to be one, and once they open their ears, they are not able to coordinate. This kind of one accord is artificial and self-made. This kind of oneness is in vain. A person may be able to shut his mouth for today and tomorrow, but two days later, he will not be able to shut his mouth any longer. Instead, "thunder" and "rain" will pour out when he opens his mouth. The oneness of the church is not like this. It is impossible to be one in the natural man, and there is no way to find oneness in the flesh and in the old creation. In other words, there is no oneness in our zeal, our diligence, our preferences, and our views. Oneness is in resurrection and in the Holy Spirit, and the Holy Spirit is in our spirit. As long as we learn not to rely on our self, our natural man, our feelings, our views, our emotions, our preferences, our ideas, and our will and learn to turn to our spirit and live in our spirit, we will have the genuine one accord. In this way we will not only have no need to grit our teeth and shut our mouths, but we will also be able to enjoy the sweetness of the one accord. If all of us would feel in our spirit, speak in our spirit, observe in our spirit, and taste in our spirit, we would have the sweet oneness. The oneness is in the spirit and in resurrection. The church is also in the spirit and in resurrection.

OUR MIND, EMOTION, AND WILL
NEEDING TO BE IN RESURRECTION

The church is not in the natural realm but in resurrection. Hence, our natural mind and emotions are problems to the church because they cannot touch resurrection. What is resurrection? Resurrection has a principle—any object that is of resurrection is not the same as it was originally. Consider a flower seed for instance. Its original shape is round and small, and its color is brownish-yellow. But after it is planted into the ground, dies, and resurrects, what comes forth is unconfined, big in shape, and green in color. This is resurrection. What is planted is the original form, but what comes out is another form. Hence, we are not saying that our mind is useless but that our mind, like a seed, has to be put to death and then to live again. Then our mind will be a mind of resurrection. Similarly, we are not saying that our emotion is useless. Spiritual men are very emotional. The difference is that if our emotion is a natural emotion, it will be a spiritual harm, but if our emotion is put to death and passes through resurrection, it will become a spiritual benefit.

In the matter of following and serving the Lord, we need a strong will. Our will has to be so strong that we are able to push forward despite repeated frustrations. This is to be spiritual. If our will is natural, it is like crude steel, having little use. However, if the steel is well-refined, it can be made into different kinds of springs for watches, being firm and at the same time pliable. After the steel is refined by fire and passes through hammering and high pressure, it is no longer crude steel but wrought steel. This steel is not only firm but pliable. The will of some people is natural and has not passed through the dealing of death. It is like crude steel that has not been forged or hammered. A will that is like crude steel is a problem to the church. Where there are such saints, there are problems. In fact, people with this kind of will are unbearable. However, if their will passes through death and enters into resurrection, the resurrected will becomes a spiritual will that is both firm and pliable and is a benefit to the church.

Our natural mind, emotion, and will have to pass through death and resurrection. How can this be accomplished? How can our mind, emotion, and will be put to death? Suppose you are a person who is rich in thoughts. When you serve in the church, it is easy for your thoughts to come out. At such times, you have to learn to reject your mind, your thoughts, and your ideas by the Holy Spirit, putting aside your mind, your thinking, and your train of thought by the Holy Spirit. This putting aside of your mind is to put it to death. If your thoughts and mind are something that God wants, after you have put them to death, God will surely raise them up. This is the same with our emotion and will.

When we are serving together with the saints, if our mind and ideas come out quickly, we have to reject them immediately. If our emotion comes out, we have to reject it in the same way. It is the same with our will; we have to reject it. We have to learn to reject all that is natural and inborn and put it aside. If we reject our mind, emotion, and will in this way and turn to our spirit, we will touch the Spirit. In the Spirit there is resurrection, and in resurrection there is the church. This is the sequence in which the church is produced not only in Christ's work but also in our experience.

In our experience, if we want to express the church in our living, we have to begin from resurrection. Again and again we have to learn to put our natural mind, emotion, and will aside, reject and deny them, and turn to the spirit. Once we turn to the spirit, we will touch the Holy Spirit, and once we touch the Holy Spirit, we will touch resurrection. In this way you will be in resurrection, I will be in resurrection, this brother will be in resurrection, and everyone will be in resurrection. What comes out of resurrection is the church. At that time what we live out will be the church, resurrection, and the oneness. This is also the fullness of Christ as the One who fills all in all. This is the Body of Christ. With this, our sweeping the floor will express the church, our preaching the gospel will express the church, our visiting people will express the church, and our praying will also express the church. Whatever we do will express the church. There will be no divisions, no sects, no opinions, no sin, no death, no world, and no flesh. Everything will be spiritual, of resurrection, and in oneness. All we will have will be just Christ Himself, the One who fills all in all.

THE CHURCH BEING FILLED UNTO
THE FULLNESS OF GOD

Ephesians 1 is concerning revelation, and chapter three is concerning experience. Regarding experience, Paul asked God to grant us the power. Seeing requires revelation, and experience requires power. Paul prayed that God would strengthen us into our inner man that we would be full of strength. In chapter one Paul showed us that Christ is in the heavenlies, but in chapter three, for our experience, he showed us that Christ is in us as the indwelling Christ.

If the electricity at the electric plant is not connected to our home, we will not be able to enjoy it. In the same way, it is possible for us to know the Christ in the heavens without experiencing or enjoying Him; for Christ to be our enjoyment and experience, He must enter into us to be the Christ in us. Regarding revelation, we have to see that Christ is in ascension. Regarding experience, we have to see that He as the indwelling Christ is in us. The Holy Spirit in us strengthens us with power that the indwelling Christ may make home in us and that we may be filled unto all the fullness of God.

Hence, the two prayers in Ephesians are not for two things but for one thing. Chapter one shows us what this thing is, and chapter three tells us how to experience it. When we are in the spirit and in resurrection, the ascended Christ whom we know in our spirit becomes the indwelling Christ. This Christ becomes our content, and we become His Body. Eventually, we will be filled unto all the fullness of God, unto the Christ who fills all in all. In other words, the Body of Christ is the mingling of God and man, and when man is filled unto the fullness of God, this is the Body of Christ.

THE CHURCH EXISTING ONLY IN RESURRECTION

Whether a person is a member of the Body of Christ, a part of the Body, all depends on whether he has God mingled with him. If he does, he is a part of the Body of Christ. But if he does not have God mingled with him, though he may be saved, he is still not a part of the Body of Christ in reality. Hence, we must learn to live in the spirit. Once we turn to our spirit, we will touch the Holy Spirit as well as resurrection. In resurrection the church and the members of the Body of Christ will surely grow up. When we live in resurrection, the ascended Christ, the Christ who is on the throne, becomes the Christ in us. Christ's being in us issues in our being filled unto all the fullness of God. This causes us to become part of the Body of Christ in reality. The Body of Christ, which is in resurrection, is the mystery in this universe.

To be in resurrection is to be in ascension, transcending over all things and being far above all things. Whenever we live in resurrection, we are not only in the realm of ascension, but we transcend over all things. At these times the problems in our coordination will not be able to touch us, the problems in our family will not be able to touch us, and the unsatisfactory circumstances in our work will not be able to touch us. None of the things on the earth will be able to touch us. We will be far above all and over all things.

There was once a brother who was dealt with by an elder and was unable to get through his feeling. This shows that he was not in resurrection but on the earth. He had not departed from the earth. If he was in the spirit and in the heavens, no

matter what the elder said or how loud his voice was, since it
would not have reached the heavens, it would not have been
able to touch him. Sometimes we may be unable to get
through regarding certain matters or even regarding certain
people. This shows that we are too close to the earth. All the
feelings of being "unable to get through" are because we are
still on the earth. This is like an airplane taking off. When an
airplane takes off, it has to fly high in the sky. Otherwise, it
will hit a high-rise building. When we "airplanes" take off, we
often either scratch the paint or break the fuselage because
we are too close to the earth. If someone requires a small
matter from us, we are not able to take it. If someone adjusts
us a bit, we find it unbearable. There is much bitterness and
complaining in us because we are not in resurrection, in
ascension, and far above all things. A person of ascension is
one who transcends over all things and is far above all things.
One who is in resurrection, regardless of how people irritate
him, cannot be touched, because he is in ascension, transcending over all things and being far above all things. Only
this is the church, and only this produces the church.

THE CHURCH BEING THE MINGLING OF GOD AND MAN

First Corinthians 15:47 says, "The first man is out of the
earth, earthy; the second man is out of heaven." This means
that whereas the first man is earthy, belonging to the earth,
the second man is out of heaven and is "resurrectionly" and
heavenly. When we live in the second man, we live in resurrection, and when we live in resurrection, we live in the
heavens. A person who lives in heaven transcends over all
things and is far above all things. This kind of person lives in
the realm of ascension and is far above all things. He has
Christ indwelling and filling him. The One who fills all in all
is in him. Such a person is filled unto all the fullness of God.
He and God, God and he, are mingled as one.

May God be merciful to us and open our eyes to see that
all these spiritual truths are not doctrines or things that are
abstract and distant. Although these truths are wonderful
and profound, their reality is in the Holy Spirit and in resurrection. If we live in resurrection, we will have the reality, and

if we live in the Holy Spirit, this reality will be expressed through us practically. According to the two prayers of Paul in Ephesians, the Lord has already given us the revelation to see these divine and spiritual riches. May the Lord grant us grace upon grace that we may experience and live faithfully in this vision that has been revealed to us and learn to continuously reject our natural man and our flesh so that we may live in the Spirit and in resurrection.

When we are in the Spirit and in resurrection, we transcend over all things and are far above all things. Then the Body of Christ, which is spiritual, heavenly, resurrectionly, and far above all things, and which is the mingling of God and man, is expressed. When the Body of Christ is fully expressed, the new heaven and new earth will come. When the church has this reality, the church is spiritual, has resurrection, has life, and is heavenly, having the taste of the new heaven and new earth. In such a realm God and man are mingled as one.

About the Author

Witness Lee was born in 1905 in northern China and raised in a Christian family. At age 19 he was fully captured for Christ and immediately consecrated himself to preach the gospel for the rest of his life. Early in his service, he met Watchman Nee, a renowned preacher, teacher, and writer. Witness Lee labored together with Watchman Nee under his direction. In 1934 Watchman Nee entrusted Witness Lee with the responsibility for his publication operation, called the Shanghai Gospel Bookroom.

Prior to the Communist takeover in 1949, Witness Lee was sent by Watchman Nee and his other co-workers to Taiwan to ensure that the things delivered to them by the Lord would not be lost. Watchman Nee instructed Witness Lee to continue the former's publishing operation abroad as the Taiwan Gospel Bookroom, which has been publicly recognized as the publisher of Watchman Nee's works outside China. Witness Lee's work in Taiwan manifested the Lord's abundant blessing. From a mere 350 believers, newly fled from the mainland, the churches in Taiwan grew to 20,000 in five years.

In 1962 Witness Lee felt led of the Lord to come to the United States, settling in California. During his 35 years of service in the U.S., he ministered in weekly meetings and weekend conferences, delivering several thousand spoken messages. Much of his speaking has since been published as over 400 titles. Many of these have been translated into over fourteen languages. He gave his last public conference in February 1997 at the age of 91.

He leaves behind a prolific presentation of the truth in the Bible. His major work, *Life-study of the Bible,* comprises over 25,000 pages of commentary on every book of the Bible from the perspective of the believers' enjoyment and experience of God's divine life in Christ through the Holy Spirit. Witness Lee was the chief editor of a new translation of the New Testament into Chinese called the Recovery Version and directed the translation of the same into English. The Recovery Version also appears in a number of other languages. He provided an extensive body of footnotes, outlines, and spiritual cross references. A radio broadcast of his messages can be heard on Christian radio stations in the United States. In 1965 Witness Lee founded Living Stream Ministry, a non-profit corporation, located in Anaheim, California, which officially presents his and Watchman Nee's ministry.

Witness Lee's ministry emphasizes the experience of Christ as life and the practical oneness of the believers as the Body of Christ. Stressing the importance of attending to both these matters, he led the churches under his care to grow in Christian life and function. He was unbending in his conviction that God's goal is not narrow sectarianism but the Body of Christ. In time, believers began to meet simply as the church in their localities in response to this conviction. In recent years a number of new churches have been raised up in Russia and in many eastern European countries.

OTHER BOOKS PUBLISHED BY
Living Stream Ministry

Titles by Witness Lee:

Titles by Watchman Nee:

Available at
Christian bookstores, or contact Living Stream Ministry
2431 W. La Palma Ave. • Anaheim, CA 92801
1-800-549-5164 • www.livingstream.com